Empowering Students Through Questioning

Empowering Students Through Questioning

A Guide for Understanding the Skills in Lesson Design and Instruction

Mario C. Barbiere, Ed.D

ROWMAN & LITTLEFIELD
Lanham • Boulder • New York • London

Published by Rowman & Littlefield
An imprint of The Rowman & Littlefield Publishing Group, Inc.
4501 Forbes Boulevard, Suite 200, Lanham, Maryland 20706
www.rowman.com

86-90 Paul Street, London EC2A 4NE, United Kingdom

British Library Cataloguing in Publication Information Available

Library of Congress Cataloging-in-Publication Data

Names: Barbiere, Mario C., author.
Title: Empowering students through questioning : a guide for understanding the skills in lesson design and instruction / Mario C. Barbiere.
Description: Lanham : Rowman & Littlefield Publishing Group, [2022] | Includes bibliographical references and index. | Summary: "Empowering Students Through Questioning examines the art of question construction so teachers can plan more effective lessons and achieve greater student engagement. Addressed is the purpose of questioning, pitfalls in developing questions, types of questions to use for assessments, and activities to use to determine question effectiveness"—Provided by publisher.
Identifiers: LCCN 2021042405 (print) | LCCN 2021042406 (ebook) | ISBN 9781475864465 (cloth) | ISBN 9781475864472 (paperback) | ISBN 9781475864489 (epub)
Subjects: LCSH: Questioning. | Lesson planning. | Effective teaching. | Motivation in education.
Classification: LCC LB1027.44 .B36 2022 (print) | LCC LB1027.44 (ebook) | DDC 371.3/7—dc23/eng/20211018
LC record available at https://lccn.loc.gov/2021042405
LC ebook record available at https://lccn.loc.gov/2021042406

This book is dedicated to all the professionals in education who go to work every day and work with students to give them hope for a bright future, help them realize their dreams, and believe in them. Each individual student will make the world a better place. Never stop believing! To the dreamers and the doers.

Contents

Preface

Having the opportunity to work for several decades in education with low-performing schools or schools with an achievement gap and completing a year of research on how kids learn, I have achieved a balance of practice and theory which is necessary to understand teaching and student learning.

I discovered that my passion was in school turnaround and student self-regulation. In both cases, they share a driving force: empowerment. With teachers, some, if not many, believe that school turnaround is a matter of "fixing" teachers. That belief never gets the desired results and, in most cases, causes more problems than it solves. As an executive director of a regional Achievement Center working for the New Jersey Department of Education, I had low-performing schools or schools with an achievement gap in seven of the twenty-one counties in New Jersey. All of my schools were able to exit "status" as the focus was on understanding the nature of the learner and developing lessons to meet their needs. More importantly, the major tenet was teacher and student empowerment. Teachers need to be empowered as well as the students so they can hone their craft. Students need to become empowered so they can self-regulate their learning and therefore become self-dependent and not teacher dependent.

Doing learning walks aka coaching walks, walk-throughs, I quickly noticed how many questions teachers asked during a lesson. It never seemed like a lot of questions until I actually kept track of the number of questions asked. Wow! There are a lot of questions that teachers asked during a lesson. That realization prompted me to develop rubrics for questioning. I spent years doing research as I wanted to develop rubrics that all teachers can use regardless of the evaluation instrument that is used to assess them. More importantly, it caused me to ask: what is the purpose of questioning? In essence, what are the students doing-listening, acting or Really, what are students doing: listening, acting, nodding their head or smiiling?

The challenge was on. Can I develop a tool that assesses teacher questions? After years of research, I did construct a tool assessing teacher questions using Revised Bloom's Taxonomy to determine the questions teachers were asking. I added to the rubric what students are doing as the result of the question asked using Webb's Depth of Knowledge. A perfect marriage: inputs and outputs! The instrument was field tested in my schools, and it was an eye-opening experience for administrators and teachers. Teachers were able to see the impact of their questioning.

One way to promote empowerment for teachers and self-regulation for students is to provide rubrics that can be used to assess progress. Rubrics are necessary for student self-regulation. Rubrics also mitigate allegations of bias as expectations are clearly delineated in the rubric. Additionally, rubrics which are standards-based maintain standards but lower the barrier as students can assess where they are and what they need to do to get to the next level. Rubrics can be used by teachers, administrators, parents, or students so everyone knows what the expectations are.

Understanding the twenty-first-century learner and how she needs to be taught to self-regulate, become autonomous, and acquire skills needed to become successful in and out of the classroom environment, the reader will have strategies for lesson design and delivery.

The book is developed starting with understanding the nature of the learner. After all, it is all about the student and the student's success. Inherent in student success is promoting student self-regulation. How many teachers know students with high IQs who go to college and fail after the first marking period because they could not self-regulate?

The subsequent chapter looks at the common pitfalls in developing questions so as not to make mistakes in the lesson planning.

Knowing what pitfalls to avoid, the teacher can plan what questions to use to promote discussion and student metacognition. The second chapter will define the following areas of lesson design as developed in the Learner's Brain Model that addresses phases of instruction: Planning, Readiness, Informational, and Closure and questions appropriate for each stage.

A chapter will be devoted to developing effective questions and activities to incorporate self-regulation principles and strategies into each phase of the instructional process, linking teacher questions to developing a growth mindset and evaluating questions for each stage of instructional delivery using the Learner's Brain Model for lesson planning and delivery.

This book is useful for administrators, teachers, parents, coaches, resource teachers, supervisors, department chairs, content specialists, behavioral or instructional coaches, interventionists, mentor teachers, peer coaches, and district content specialists. They can use the information to target specific skills or deficiencies, to model lessons, or as a professional improvement plan resource.

Why not take the journey?

Acknowledgments

I have come to realize that success is sweet when it is achieved through teamwork and collaboration. As such, I have been fortunate to lead a team of educators that were charged with turning around low-performing schools in the state of New Jersey as part of a pilot program implementing Regional Achievement Center. As executive director for Regional Achievement Center 5, I was fortunate to have a great team and we were able to have all of our schools exit "status" of being labeled as a "focus school". Over a career spanning five decades, the five years I worked for the state of New Jersey were by far my most enjoyable years.

Thanks to Ms. Shelia Wegryn, Mr. Michael Littlejohn, Mr. William Anderson, Ms. Neyda Evans, Dr. Fran Borkes, Dr. Jean Voorhees, Ms. Ilium Okum. Dr. Joann Berkley, and Mr. Frank Zalocki for all your help and support over the years. We had great success that included some laughs in the process. It was an honor to lead such a talented team of educators.

Doing the work of school turnaround has been exciting and personally rewarding. It was made rewarding by the spirit of cooperation from the teachers, assistant principals, supervisors, principals, central office administrators, and superintendents that I worked with in the seven counties in New Jersey.

Thank you to Ms. Jane Waitr for pushing me and for your help and support.

Thank you as well to Tom Koerner and your staff at Rowman & Littlefield for making my dream become a reality.

To all the teachers involved in school turnaround who believe and make student dreams come true, your efforts are acknowledged and appreciated. Believe in students, and they will "see" it and achieve the success that we all want for our scholars. We never want to extinguish hopes and dreams as that may be the only thing one has.

Finally, to my sons who give me purpose and light up my life, and to Kermie for molding me into who I am. You are missed but the vision carries on.

Introduction

This book is organized to follow a natural progression from the teacher to the learner and the types of questions teachers can use for assessing student knowledge. Having been involved in school turnaround, the key to success is to have teachers understand the purpose. Once teachers (and administrators) understand the purpose, they can frame the information they are learning, and contextualize the data so it becomes meaningful. Every teacher understands this principle quickly when a student asks one of two questions: "Is this going to be on the test?" (In other words, why are we learning this?) or "Why do I have to learn this?" (In other words, this information serves no purpose).

Accordingly, this book begins with understanding purpose. The first chapter asks the question: *What is the purpose of questioning?* The chapter begins with understanding the purpose of questioning. Once the purpose is identified, teachers will know the pitfalls to avoid in order to ensure that their questions are effective.

To help guide the teacher's attention while reading the chapter, there are three focus questions that are posed:

1. How do teachers plan their questioning?
2. What are the different pitfalls to avoid when developing questions?
3. What are strategies a teacher can use for whole-class participation?

The second chapter builds on the first chapter by focusing on questioning pitfalls. Once teachers know the purpose of questioning, what pitfalls can they avoid to ensure that their questions are effective? In planning the questions for a lesson, the teacher must be mindful of which pitfalls occur in the lesson planning. The lessons must be planned carefully to ensure that the level of questioning is appropriate for the students, varied, and purposeful for a desired end. Lessons that incorporate questions should be posed to promote learning. Knowing and understanding questioning pitfalls to avoid when designing questions will be necessary for integrating questions in the teacher's lesson planning.

Chapter 3 takes the reader to the next level of questioning development by determining what questions should be included in instructional delivery. This chapter is extremely important as teachers are at various levels of proficiency in their practice and may have had training in developing questions or knowing the different types of questions but understanding what questions to use is the key to effective questioning. This chapter focuses on question selection for instructional delivery. It answers the question: "What types of questions should I use and what instructional approach should I employ?" The focus of the chapter is:

1. What instructional delivery should I use?
2. What kinds of questions should I ask to get the most out of the lesson?
3. What kinds of questions should I use for whole-group and small-group questioning?

The chapter will provide strategies for the teacher for planning her questions to use before, during, and after instruction as each phase of the instructional process will require different types of questions and as each phase of instruction has a different purpose. The "before" phase is consistent with the Learner's Brain Model developed by Dr. Barbiere (2018). The Learner's Brain Model involves four stages: Planning, Readiness, Informational, and Closure.

After reviewing the first chapter about the nature of the learners, the following chapter discusses pitfalls in developing questions. The following chapter shares strategies in using questions in the instructional approach and focuses the reader attention to answering a simple question:

1. What is an effective question?
2. When are the different types of questions necessary?
3. How can a teacher determine if her questions are effective?

To prompt the teacher's reflection, the author asks: Have you ever wondered why a question that you were asked is one of your favorite questions? Perhaps the question was something you were expecting or hoping to be asked so your anticipation of the question finally came? There are specific questions that are tailored for desired results. As teachers, we can plan our questions because we know the desired goal we are trying to achieve, so our questions can bring a student to the level we are seeking. This chapter investigates the various types of questions and the desired results from them.

When teachers plan their lessons, there are activities and strategies they can use to plan the kinds of questions to use as well as to assess their effectiveness. The frame of reference in the lesson planning will be developing student self-regulation and promoting a growth mind-set mentality for the student. The outline of this chapter will be to use the four stages of the Learner's Brain Model, developed by Dr. Barbiere as a template for the lesson plan. Details about the Learner's Brain Model can be found in two books by Dr. Barbiere: *Setting the Stage: Delivering the Plan Using the Learner's Brain Model* and *Activating the Learner's Brain: Using the Learner's Brain Model.*

This chapter specifically follows other chapters because the previous chapters ask the teacher to reflect on the types of questioning that are planned and used. The focus of this chapter is for the teacher to start to develop questioning activities to promote student self-regulation and development of a growth mind-set. This chapter is very important to educators as the goal of all teachers is to promote student self-regulation so the student becomes empowered and able to regulate their learning. This chapter is a must-read chapter in the book as it gets to the heart of student empowerment and developing self-regulation strategies for learners. There are three focus questions posed:

1. How will the teacher incorporate self-regulation principles and strategies into each phase of the instructional process?
2. How can teachers link their questions for developing a growth mind-set?
3. How can teachers evaluate their questions for each stage of instructional delivery using the Learner's Brain Model for lesson planning and delivery?

A critical aspect of instructional delivery is assessment. How effective was the lesson or more importantly, how does a teacher know the lesson was effective? As teachers develop assessments, what kind of questions should be used and more importantly, what type of assessments are most desirable for achieving a specific goal? For example, if the teacher wants to determine if a student understands facts, then a multiple-choice type of test would be an effective way for the student to show her knowledge of facts.

This chapter examines the various types of assessments that can be used depending on the desired results the teacher is seeking. This chapter will focus on strategies and activities to determine question effectiveness. The chapter answers the question: When does a teacher use (1) multiple choice, (2) true/false, (3) matching, (4) short answer, or (5) essay assessments, and what activities can be used to determine question effectiveness? These questions will help teachers prepare appropriate assessments to use.

Finally, the last chapter will show a sample lesson and include questions that can be used in a lesson and the types of assessments to use so teachers can see how instruction and assessment are tied together. The lesson is written using the Learner's Brain Model developed by Dr. Barbiere.

This book addresses empowering teachers in lesson design and instruction and provides strategies for students to use to self-regulate their learning. A must-read for novice to experienced teachers so they will know what types of questions to use and how their questioning can promote student self-regulation.

Chapter 1

Purpose of Questioning

TEXTBOX 1.1

What is the focus of this chapter?

This chapter will answer the question: What is the purpose of questioning? Once the purpose is identified, what are questions I should ask myself for planning a lesson?

Focus Questions:

1. What is the role of questioning and teacher evaluations?
2. Why do I ask questions?
3. What are my planning questions?

INTRODUCTION: WHAT IS YOUR FAVORITE QUESTION?

"To be or not to be" is probably one of the more famous questions that had been asked. What was the best question that you were asked? Was it: Do you want to go out on a date? Will you marry me? Where do you want to go on vacation? Did we win the lottery? (That will be the best question if the answer is yes.) Should we get a new car? What kind? There are so many questions that are your favorite question based on the fact that you were hoping to be asked that specific question. So, the real question is: What was that particular question your favorite question? Is it because you were hoping that it would be asked and you were ready for it and had the answer ready? Or, is it your favorite question because you were surprised that the question was asked? In either case, the question that was asked was important to you.

The value of questioning is important in how they are asked, how they create a frame of reference or are used to get one to a desired level. So, let's look at the value of questioning but first start at the beginning.

Where Do We Begin: The Socratic Method?

Perhaps one would attribute the questioning process to the Socrates whose significant contribution to Western thought was his method of inquiry, known as the Socratic method or method of "elenchus." He used questions to examine key moral concepts via posing a series of questions to determine their beliefs and the extent of knowledge. Based on the response, he scaffolded his questions. Regrettably, Socrates did not write any of his work but his work was first described by Plato in the *Socratic Dialogues*. One can only wonder what it would be like to have his work published in a book to read firsthand what he had to say.

To solve a problem, Socrates would ask a series of questions. This process is one that is effectively used today, or at least in some cases used effectively today. The initial purpose of the questions would be to assess the person's knowledge or belief system. He would scaffold the questions to bring the person or group to a gradual understanding of their own beliefs on the subject to help them draw a conclusion. The development and practice of this method of discussion and questioning is a contribution attributed to Socrates but since he did not leave writings, we have to rely on the work of Plato or Xenophon.

To illustrate the use of the Socratic method, the process begins by posing a series of questions to a person or a group to determine their underlying belief system and philosophical base. As teachers use factual questions in a lesson to determine what their students know, the goal being to get an understanding of the student's starting point. Socrates questioning would serve a similar purpose. Subsequently, a baseline is discovered, faulty hypothesis can be eliminated via questioning and the person comes to a new understanding. By eliminating faulty hypothesis, a strong and better hypothesis can be constructed. In essence, the person has come to a new understanding through what she perceives is her own understanding.

How Do We Go from Socrates to the Classroom?

Many teacher evaluation instruments encourage teacher questioning. Stronge (2012) lists Performance Standard 3 as Instructional Delivery and engaging and maintaining students in active learning. He cites research that teachers promotes teachers using multiple levels of questioning aligned with student's cognitive abilities.

Danielson (2013) also promotes questioning as her Domain 3: Instruction has as an indicator 3b: Using questioning and Discussion Techniques. Questioning and discussion are the only instructional strategies specifically referred to in the Framework for Teaching because questions of high-quality cause students to think and reflect, deepen their understanding and to test their ideas against those of their classmates. Danielson's philosophy is that effective teachers promote learning through discussion. This foundational skill that students learn is through engaging in discussion by explaining and justifying their reasoning and conclusions, based on specific evidence. Teachers skilled in the use of questioning and discussion techniques challenge students to examine their premises, to build a logical argument, and to critique the arguments of others—the same concept that Socrates promoted.

The McREL teacher evaluation system, Standard 3 states: "teachers know the content they teach. Teachers are rated distinguished when they: Deepen student understanding of 21st century skills and helps them make their own connections and develop new skills" (McREL, 2010). The indicators include:

- Require students to take responsibility for their own learning.
- Have students defend decisions for open-ended real-world questions.
- Develop student-designed rubrics for evaluating personal responsibility.
- Use actual court cases, political debates, legislative actions to enhance instruction.
- Allow students opportunities to self-select projects emphasizing twenty-first-century skills

Questioning plays a big part in teacher evaluations as it is the questions that promote metacognition and discussion. How does the teacher know that the student knows the material? What questions must the teacher ask to assess student knowledge? More importantly, what questions promote metacognition or do all questions promote knowledge?

What Promotes Knowledge?

Administrators who observe teachers will see teachers asking questions and/ or students asking questions. So, how is classroom knowledge determined? Alison Jones (1981), a researcher in New Zealand, described and named an instance of student control over what counts as classroom knowledge by studying a classroom and teacher questioning. Was the teacher's focus on her questioning from the vantage point of "student control." Did the teacher use higher-level thinking about their subject since the teacher presumed that higher-level thinking would promote greater student cognition and that consequently students would do better on the high stakes testing? To the researcher's surprise, the students wanted facts so they could have the facts as part of their notes so they could remember the facts and do well in the test (Manke, 2001, in Collins et al., 2001).

The question now becomes: Does the test determine the kinds of questions that teachers will use? That question will be explored in detail in chapter 4, "Developing Effective Questions." Let's look at some of the reasons teachers ask questions so we can determine if the questions being asked are effective.

Why Do Teachers Ask Questions in Class?

Perhaps the concept of questioning is more a requirement as states that have adopted the Common Core State Standards have standards for each discipline and in the standards questioning is required to meet the standard. For example, the English Language Arts (ELA) standards include speaking and listening with reading and writing. The belief of the ELA standard is that the skills support and reinforce each other and are interdependent. The focus is threefold: (1) to engage effectively in a range of collaborative discussions on a one-on-one basis, in groups, and teacher-led; (2) to pose and respond to specific questions with elaboration and detail by making comments that contribute to the topic, text, or issue under discussion; and (3) to propel conversations by posing and responding to questions that relate the current discussion to broader themes or ideas, actively incorporating others into the discussion and clarifying, verifying, or challenging ideas and conclusions (Common Core State Standards. Available http://www.corestandards.org/ELA-Literacy).

As per the Common Core Standards of Mathematical Practice students are required to "justify their conclusions, communicate them to others, and respond to the arguments and ask useful questions of others" and that "students at all grades listen or read the arguments of others, decide whether they make sense, and ask useful questions to clarify or improve the arguments" (Common Core State Standards. Available at: (www.corestandards/Math/Practice).

Effective Mathematical discourse suggestions in Principles of Actions (National Council of Teachers of Mathematics (2014), lists eight effective teaching practices. The practices described that helps teachers engage students in the habits of mind highlighted in the Mathematical Practices (Common Core State Standards, 2010) include:

1. Establish mathematical goals that focus learning.
2. Implement tasks that promote reasoning and problem solving.
3. Use and connect mathematical representations.

4. Facilitate meaningful mathematical discourse.
5. Pose purposeful questions.
6. Build procedural fluency from conceptual understanding.
7. Support productive struggle in learning mathematics.
8. Elicit and use evidence of student thinking.

In addition to the eight practices, Mathematical Discourse suggests three talk moves to engage students: individual Think Time (ITT), turn and Talk, and The Four Rs—repeat, rephrase, reword, and record. The critical purpose of the three moves is meant to engage the students in mathematical discourse and, more importantly, focus on helping students make sense rather than answering questions or "answer telling." Herein lies the value of questioning: How to promote student thinking and how to promote "making sense" of the material? Those questions will be addressed in chapter 4: "Effective Questioning."

Individual "Think Time" is an action a teacher takes which is deliberate and purposeful. It is a quiet pause that allows students to interpret a question. Teachers know it as "wait-time" as they are for the students to recollect his or her thoughts before moving on. The task is to model the strategy so students will use it in student-to-student talk. Individual "Think Time" may sometimes be 10 seconds which is considerably longer than teacher wait-time of 3–5 seconds. In many cases, 3–5 seconds seems like a lifetime to teachers! At an extreme end it can sometimes be much longer than 10 seconds and last a minute or two, depending on the complexity of the task and the thinking required to make sense of it. The purpose of wait-time is to allow each and every student to enter a discussion about mathematical concepts that will be shared. It provides processing time for students to make sense of what they are looking at or what they just heard and begin to formulate their own thinking in relation to it. This practice is probably a good practice for any question asking employed by teachers.

In the area of Science, Next Generation Science Standards (NGSS) has four of the eight science practices directly related to questioning or discussion; asking questions: constructing and explanations; engaging in arguments from evidence; and obtaining evaluating and communicating information.

The Science Standards promote asking questions and defining problems. For the study of Heredity, S-L.S5-1), questions are used to assess data; in for Earth and Human Activity (MS-ESS3-5) questions are used to assess data; for energy (MS-PS3-3) questions are asked to predict outcomes; for Motion and Stability; Forces and Interactions (PS2-3), are used to determine cause and effect relationship.

Questioning becomes critical for addressing the standards because it promotes metacognition.

How Important Is Questioning?

Questioning is regarded as an integral part of the teaching and the learning process especially since all of the standards require questioning. Even more important is the value of questioning as teachers spend a lot of time asking questions. Research has shown that teachers ask a high frequency of questions. In 1967, Schreiber found that fifth-grade teachers asked about sixty-four questions each during thirty-minute social studies lessons. Floyd (1960) developed a study with forty elementary teachers and found that these teachers asked 93 percent of all classroom questions. These numbers confirm the results obtained by Stevens in her precursor study about classroom questioning conducted in 1912. More recently, Kerry (2002) reinforces these numbers referring that if teachers ask an average of 43.6 questions per hour, in an average career they are likely to ask about 2 million questions. That is a lot of questions? Isn't it?

Early research on teacher questioning behaviors and patterns indicate that teachers spend approximately 80 percent of the school day asking as many as 300–400 questions to students (Stevens, 1912; Leven & Long, 1981). However, some contemporary educators spend a more conservative 35–50 percent of their instructional time asking questions.

Let's look at the reason why teachers ask questions.

Why Do Teachers Ask Questions?

Teacher questioning is a major part of the teacher's instructional delivery protocol. In fact, researchers note that verbal questioning is second only to lecturing as the most common instructional practice (Black, 2001). Teachers ask about 300–400 questions per day and as many as 120 questions per hour. Think about it—120 questions per hour is a lot of questions. So one has to wonder what the wait time is like between the questions. More importantly, are there student questions that are posed during this time period? If so, how does the teacher plan for student questioning in the lesson planning? Or, more importantly, does she plan for student questioning in the lesson?

Let's see why teachers ask questions. Perhaps some reasons are included in table 1.1.

What Are Questions to Ask Yourself about Your Questioning?

Refer to Barbiere, M. (2018). *Setting the Stage: Delivering the Plan Using the Learner's Brain Model*, MD: Rowman & Littlefield.

What Are My Planning Questions?

Now that I have information from my students, I can plan my questions to use for my next lesson. Starting with the Planning Stage of the Learner's

Table 1.1 Purpose and Rationale of Factual Type Questions

Question Type: Factual	Purpose	Rationale
What do you think? Who, what, when, where, how types of questions. What does it mean?	To promote student engagement. Promote student metacognition? Develop student knowledge?	Actually, teachers sometimes think compliance is engagement. Engagement refers to the student's cognition as a result of the question that was asked. So, to promote engagement, the question posed by teachers requires student cognition about the recall level. In essence: What are the students doing as a result of the questions posed?
Can you give me an example? Can you show, paraphrase, summarize, distinguish, or demonstrate x?	Student involvement.	Open-ended questions are more inclined to promote discussion as opposed to closed questions. Asking students to show, summarize, or paraphrase encourages them to think about what they are reading or listening to and to justify their response with cognition.
How many students agree with x?	Check for understanding used to assess student knowledge.	Checks for understandings are used to assess what students know so the teacher can monitor and adjust the lesson.
Questions: Concepts (conceptual knowledge) Analyze.	Purpose Questions are used to promote a conceptual understanding of the topic.	Rationale How will the question help the student piece the facts into broader concepts? Once students know facts, they can piece the facts together to understand the broader concepts? By asking students to analyze and compare the student will show her understanding of the concept.
Compare and contrast types of questions. Justify if the information is a fact or an opinion.	Application of facts	Students take individual or isolated facts and weave them together into concepts. This promotes the student's ability to see relationships and weave them together into broader concepts. Being able to see horizontal relationships and dig deeper vertically to tie the horizontal pieces onto a vertical web.
Questions: Process (procedural knowledge)	Purpose	Rationale

(Continued)

Table 1.1 Purpose and Rationale of Factual Type Questions (*Continued*)

Question Type: Factual	Purpose	Rationale
Justify, evaluate. Find an equation to solve this problem. How do you know it is correct? Please explain.	Different from declarative knowledge which is explicit, procedural knowledge is performed by doing as opposed to different from what was stated?	This is also known as imperative knowledge which is the knowledge that is practiced through the performance of tasks. This knowledge enables the person to know how and when they should apply the information attained.
How . . .	Procedural knowledge differs from declarative knowledge, which is thought of as "knowledge about" or the answers to the what, where, when, or who types of questions, rather than the "how."	Develop reasoning, problem solving, and critical thinking. The application of the concepts becomes second nature or automated.
"What would happen if . . ." questions.	Have students make predictions, estimations, or hypotheses, and design ways to test them.	Engage students to challenge assumptions, share ideas, and think outside the box.
Questions: Product. (Metacognition for creation) Ask questions that allow learners to reflect on their own learning processes and strategies. Have them practice "oral rehearsal" and share their thinking.	Purpose To take information and the information. Have students practice oral rehearsal to share their thinking.	Rationale Promote student self-regulation. Metacognitive skills are more effective when tied to a specific content.

Table 1.2   Information taken for Dr Barbiere's Learners Brain Model (2018)

Planning Stage*
1. Did I collect data for planning this lesson?
2. Is the data used for this lesson or to supplement or enrich lessons?
3. Will I plan self-regulation strategies in the lesson?
4. Will I set the "mood" of the classroom so it is conductive for question seeking by students?
5. Is the SLT tied to standards?
6. Do I need to review my classroom rules prior to the instruction?
7. Am I planning for the lesson to make sense to the students?
8. Am I planning to ensure that the lesson has meaning to the students?
9. Will I plan application of the skills into the lesson?

Readiness Stage
1. Does the verb in the SLT promote cognition?
2. Are the nouns that I use tied to the knowledge I am seeking?
3. Is the target going to be measurable?
4. Is the SLT part of a short-term learning goal?
5. Is the SLT tied to standards?
6. Does the assessment of the SLT include multiple means?
7. Will there be an essential question used?
8. Will the lesson be rigorous?
9. Will data be collected during the lesson to assess progress?

Informational Stage
1. Will I plan a multisensory approach in the lesson?
2. Will the lesson be standards based and rigorous?
3. Have I planned an activity to activate prior knowledge?
4. Do I have measurable learning outcomes (DSL)?
5. Did I plan a closure activity for the class to get feedback?
6. Do I have questions planned throughout the lesson?
7. Do I have questions planned to scaffold the lesson?

Closure Stage
1. Do I have a purpose for a closure activity?
2. Have I planned an activity to assess the lesson being taught?
3. Will I use an overt closure activity?
4. Will I use a covert closure activity?
5. Will I use the information from closure to plan tomorrow's lesson?

Brain Model, it is suggested that the planning begins with analyzing the data to determine where the students are and what needs to be reviewed, re-taught before the new lesson can proceed. Once that data is determined based on the student's needs, the new lesson can be planned. The new lesson can be scaffolded based on the data.

For the Planning Stage:

- What does the data tell me?
- How will the data help me differentiate my lesson?
- Will I plan what questions to ask?
- How will I ensure learning will occur?

For the Readiness Stage

- What verbs will I use to promote cognition in my Student Learning Target (SLT)?
- What knowledge do I want the students to know?
- How will I promote student interest?
- What questions will I use to focus student interest?
- What questions will I use to make sense and have meaning?

Instructional Stage

- Am I planning gradual release?
- How will independent learning be monitored?
- How will I promote student self-regulation? What questions will I use to prompt or cue students for self-regulation?
- What kinds of questions will I use to scaffold the lesson?
- What kinds of questions will I use to monitor the lesson?
- How will I balance teacher questions and student questions throughout the lesson?
- Will I use a mixture of low-level questions and high-level questions?

Closure Stage

- What kind of closure am I planning?
- What prompts will I use for closure?
- What will I do with information I gain from closure?

SUMMARY

Teachers plan lessons using many sources of data. The data is collected during and after the lesson and that information is used to plan subsequent lessons. What is not usually planned are the questions that will be asked. The planning of questions is critically important as teachers ask hundreds of questions during the course of the day and more importantly, the 40–60 questions during the course of a lesson. With that number of questions being asked, the teacher can ask fewer questions but will be very specific and require more planning. Additionally, the teacher can plan questions based on a specific purpose. Knowing the purpose will enable teachers to know the kinds of questions to ask.

The next chapter will address pitfalls teachers will encounter when they are developing their questioning.

REFERENCES

Albergaria-Almeida, P. (2010). Classroom questioning: Teacher's perceptions and practices. *Procedia Social and Behavioral Sciences*. Received October 5, 2009; revised December 14, 2009; accepted January 4, 2010. Retrieved from https://pdf .sciencedirectassets.com.

Alvermann, D. E. (1991). The discussion web: A graphic aid for learning across the curriculum. *The Reading Teacher, 45*(2), 92–99.

Anderson, L., & Krathwohl, D. (Eds.). (2001). *A taxonomy for learning, teaching, and assessing: A revision of Bloom's taxonomy of educational objectives*. New York: Addison Wesley Longman.

Applebee, A., Langer, J., Nystrand, M., & Gamoran, A. (2003). Discussion-based approaches to developing understanding: Classroom instruction and student performance in middle and high school English. *American Educational Research Journal, 40*, 685–730.

Beck, I., McKeown, M., & Hamilton, R. (n.d.). (2013). *Questioning the author: An approach for enhancing student engagement with text*. Newark, DE: International Reading Association.

Betts, G. H. (1910). *The recitation*. Boston: Houghton-Mifflin.

Bloom, B. S. (1987). *Taxonomy of educational objectives. Book 1: Cognitive domain*. New York: Longman.

Bransford, J., Brown, A., & Cocking, R. (Eds.). (2000). *How people learn: Brain, mind, experience and school*. Washington, DC: National Academy Press.

Cawelti, G. (1999). *Handbook of research on improving student achievement* (2nd ed.). Arlington, VA: Educational Research Service.

Clark, A. M., Anderson, R. C., Kuo, L. J., Kim, I. H., Archodidou, A., & Nguyen-Jahiel, K. (2003). Collaborative reasoning: Expanding ways for children to talk and think in school. *Educational Psychology Review, 15*(2), 181–198.

Common Core State Standards. Retrieved from http://www.corestandards.org/ELA -Literacy

Corley, M. A., & Rauscher, C. (2013). *Deeper learning through questioning, TEAL center fact sheet no. 12: Deeper learning through questioning*. The Teaching Excellence in Adult Literacy (TEAL) Center is a project of the U.S. Department of Education, Office of Vocational and Adult Education (OVAE).

Cotton, K. (2000). *The schooling practices that matter most.* Portland, OR: Northwest Regional Educational Laboratory and Alexandria, VA.

Danielson, C. (2013). The framework for teaching evaluation instrument. It is available in PDF format from the Danielson Group website: www.danielsongroup.org.

Floyd, W. D. (1960). An analysis of the oral questioning activities in selected Colorado classrooms. Ph.D. Thesis. Colorado: Colorado State College.

Gallagher, J. J., & Aschner, M. J. (1963). A preliminary re- port on analyses of classroom instruction. *Merrill-Palmer Quarterly, 9*, 183–194.

Gibbons, P. (2002). *Scaffolding language, scaffolding learning.* Portsmouth, NH: Heinemann.

Kerry, T. (2002). *Explaining and questioning.* London: Nelson Thorne.

Levin, T., & Long, R. (1981). *Effective instruction.* Washington, DC: Association for Supervision and Curriculum Development.

Manke, M. (2001). Defining classroom knowledge; the part that children play. In J. Collins, K. Insley, & J. Soler (eds.) *Developing pedagogy in researching practice* (p. 26). London, England: Paul Chapman Publishing Ltd.

Manke, Mary Phillips (1997). *Classroom power relations: Understanding student-teacher interaction.* Mahwah, NJ: Lawrence Erlbaum Associates.

Marzano, R. J., Pickering, D., & McTighe, J. (1993). *Assessing student outcomes: Performance assessment using the dimensions of learning model.* Alexandria, VA: ASCD.

Mercer, N., & Dawes, L. (2014). The study of talk between teachers and students, from the 1970s until the 2010s. *Oxford Review of Education, 40*(4), 430–445. DOI: 10.1080/03054985.2014.934087

Nystrand, M. (1997). *Opening dialogue: Understanding the dynamics of language and learning in the English class-room.* New York: Teachers College Press.

Nystrand, M., Gamoran, A., & Heck, M. J. (1993). Using small groups for response to and thinking about literature. *The English Journal, 82*(1), 14–22. Schreiber, J. E. (1967). Teachers' question-asking techniques in social studies. Ph.D. Thesis. Iowa: University of Iowa.

Schweigert, W. (1991). Classroom talk: Knowledge development, and writing. *Research in the Teaching of English, 25*(4), 469–496.

Smagorinsky, P., & O'Donnell-Allen, C. (1998). Reading as mediated and mediating action: Composing meaning for literature through multimedia interpretive texts. *Reading Research Quarterly, 33*(2), 198–226.

Stevens, R. (1912). *The question as a measure of efficiency in instruction: A critical study of classroom practice.* New York: Teachers College, Columbia University.

Stronge, J. H. (2003). *Educational specialist evaluation.* Larchmont, NY: Eye on Education.

Stronge, J. H. (2010). *Evaluating what good teachers do: Eight research-based standards for assessing teacher excellence.* Larchmont, NY: Eye on Education.

Waters, T., Cameron, G., Williams, J., Dean, C., Eck, J., Davis, T., & Woempner, C. (2010). *McREL teacher evaluation system.* Denver, CO: McREL.

Wells, G. (1999). *Dialogic inquiry: Towards a sociocultural practice and theory of education.* Cambridge, England: Cambridge University Press.

Chapter 2

Pitfalls

TEXTBOX 2.1

What is the Focus of this Chapter?

Once we know the purpose of questioning, what pitfalls can we avoid to ensure that the questions are effective?

Focus Questions:

1. How do we plan our questioning?
2. What are the different pitfalls to avoid when we develop our questions?
3. What are strategies I can use for whole-class participation?

INTRODUCTION: HOW DO WE PLAN OUR QUESTIONS

Once the purpose of questions is understood, teachers can use that information to plan effective questions. In planning the questions, the teacher has to be mindful of pitfalls which can occur in the lesson planning. The lessons have to be planned carefully to ensure that the level of questioning is appropriate for the students, varied, and purposeful for a desired end. Lessons that incorporate questions should be purposeful and promote learning. Let's look at the pitfalls to avoid when designing questions.

What Are the Different Pitfalls (from A to Z) to Avoid When We Develop Our Questions?

The format for sharing pitfalls will be an alphabetical listing of the pitfalls and list a resolution for the pitfall.

Asking Too Many Questions: The tendency is for the teacher to ask a question and once the teacher gets an answer, ask another question. This usually happens when the teacher is asking factual questions, that is, who, what, how, where, when list, what do you recall, describe, select, copy, or match. Even if teachers ask a huge number of questions per class, the questions posed are usually of the same kind. Teachers ask typically low-level questions, requiring mainly memory. The author developed a form to record the questions that teachers ask and many questions are low-cognitive-level questions. The fact has been verified in all school levels (from elementary to high) and in a variety of subject areas.

Alternative: Plan your questions carefully and deliberately so the questions that are asked will be focused and meaningful. Wait for student response and then ask students to respond to the question rather than continuing with more questions.

Asking Closed Questions: There is a tendency to ask too many closed questions which need only a short answer. The problem is that since the answer is yes, no, or short, or there is only one "right" answer, it provides an opportunity for the teacher to ask more questions. On the plus side, closed questions are useful in checking pupils' memory and recall of facts. So, if the teacher wants to see the knowledge base of the students so as to scaffold the lesson beginning with the student's knowledge base.

Alternate: Use closed questions if you are going to plot the student answers. For example: Do you think that the website I provided was useful? The yes or no answers provided to the teacher will be valuable feedback to the teacher (See table 2.1.)

Another strategy is to establish an optimum length of response by saying something like "I don't want an answer of less than 10 words."

Assuming an Answer: "Does everyone understand?" "Most students will not reply as they do not want to feel "stupid" by admitting that they did not know the answer. Instead, it is much easier for the student to nod her head or smile like the rest of her classmates (See table 2.2.)

Asking a Question and Answering It Yourself: In an effort to move a lesson along, a teacher will sometimes ask factual questions. If the lesson is not moving along fast enough, the teacher will answer the questions that are asked. A collateral pitfall to a teacher answering her own questions is the teacher does not allow pupils time to think because they are already answered!

Table 2.1 Examples of closed ended questions and Open-ended questions

Closed-ended Question Example	Open-ended Question Example
Did you agree with the author?	What points did you agree with the author?
Would you go on a trip like the author?	Why would you go to x?
Did you get the correct answer to the math problem?	Describe and justify the process you used to get your answer?
Are you interested in buying a product/service today?	Why are you looking for a product/service today?
Did you like the setting of the story?	How would you describe the setting of the story?
Did you find what you were looking for today?	How can I help you find what you are looking for today?

Alternate: Know the questions that you are going to ask and determine how many factual questions are really needed. Remember to build in wait-time so you can give pupils a chance to respond. You can encourage wait-time by telling students that you are giving them time to answer questions so they can think about their answers. If you tell the students that you are allowing for wait-time, they will not be surprised when you are quiet waiting for a response. Or, you can tell the students: "think about your answer and I'll wait a few seconds for you to respond."

Asking Affirmative Statement As a Question: "Does everyone understand?" Most students will reply in the affirmative to the question: "Does everyone understand?" If someone does not agree, they probably do not want to stand out as being the only person who does not agree. The only difference is that teachers may ask: "Does everyone agree?" as a check for understanding. If she does, then she would ask the class to give her a signal: it could be a thumbs up (if the students agree), thumbs down (if the students do not agree), or thumbs midway (if the students are not sure).

Alternate: Have students share their thinking: "What resonated with you?", "Tell me what you learned today?", "Who has a question they would like to share with the class?" The goal is to have students share their thinking and/or engage in meaningful conversations.

Calling On a Single Student Prior to Asking a Question: Sometimes to get a student's attention, or to focus a student's attention a teacher will call on a student and ask the student a question: "Sandy, what was the plot of the story we just read?" Sometimes a teacher will have to focus a student's attention by calling their name. The problem with that approach is that once the teacher calls on a student, other students do not focus.

Alternate: Present the question first, wait, and then call on a student. Another approach would be to tell the class that you will not be calling on

Table 2.2   Open(divergent) and closed (convergent) questions

Increase student response time by—	Decrease student response time by—
Open, divergent questions that encourage the students to analyze, synthesize, and evaluate material. Use words like "Compare and contrast," "Explain," "Support," "Create," and "Predict and justify."	Asking closed questions that have a "yes" or "no" response. "Does everyone agree?" "Did everyone get x as an answer?" A yes or no question or a question that requires recall of a definition and/or information will not promote metacognition or robust discussion.
After you pose your question, let the student think about the response and have a long "wait-time" so students can process the question in their minds. A short wait-time is less than a second before more rapid-fire questions are posed. (They are usually more factual types of questions, hence the reason why teachers can ask so many questions during a lesson. Three to five seconds is a longer wait-time.)	Having many factual questions planned limits student response or having a short wait-time between questions because the teacher has a time constraint.
Asking students to elaborate on their answers and asking students "why?"	Telling students their answer is wrong and not asking them to think about why it is wrong.
Allow opportunities for students to pose questions amongst themselves.	Straight lecture without student interaction.
Providing opportunities that challenge students' original conceptual understandings.	Providing opportunities that do not encourage creative and critical thinking.
Encouraging students to work through their decision making process, even if it brings frustration and makes them leave their comfort zone of learning.	Giving students direct answers to their questions without allowing them to think through the decision making process

volunteers as participation is not an option. Additionally, if you tell the student that you will not be calling on volunteers, you are putting them on notice that they have to pay attention in class because anyone can be called on in class. In essence, you will be doing "cold calls." Research on cold calls indicates that when cold calling is done as a matter of teacher protocol environments and done regularly, more students participate voluntarily; the number of students participating voluntarily increased over time and more questions are asked and answered (Dallimore et al., 2012). An additional benefit was that more students participated in class discussion when cold-calling was an accepted and used practice in the classroom. The most interesting point of the research is that the comfort level in high classrooms that did cold-calling was no different in classrooms that did not do cold-calling.

Giving Multiple Sets of Directions or Providing Additional Directions as the Students Work On a Project: Today we are going to learn about the solar system and we will start by working in pairs to do research. You will have fifteen minutes to work in groups of three. Find your partners and begin to work. As students are walking around looking for partners, the teacher announces that there will be worksheets for the students to complete at the end of their fifteen-minute independent period. Finally, you will also have to develop a list of resources.

Alternate: Class, today we are going to learn about the solar system. You will work in groups of threes to do research about the project. During the research, you will be asked to make a list of three websites you recommend to your classmates. You will also have to complete a worksheet by the end of the period. I suggest you get the worksheet to refer to while you do your research. Ok, let's begin.

Rationale: Students should know what is expected of them and knowing what needs to be done will help them plan appropriately. Providing multiple instructions throughout the lesson interrupts their workflow; if the workflow is interrupted, it takes time to get back on track so provide all the instructions and let the students get to work.

Focusing On the Wrong Points/Ignoring Important Terms: Sometimes in the process of questioning, teachers ask a lot of questions. During a classroom observation, I use a rubric I developed to keep track of teacher questions. During a learning walk-through, which was 8–10 minutes of duration, one teacher asked twenty-five recall questions. In her mind, all of the recall questions were necessary to help the students have background information. But, in reality, it was rapid firing questioning which does not have the desired effect being sought.

In order for learning to go to long-term memory, metacognition requires talking or action. To promote talking, the teacher would need to ask analytical type of questions so students apply the facts.

Rationale: Metacognition requires students to apply what they know so having factual knowledge is important but applying facts is more important.

Possible Solution: Focus on questions that encourage students to think further about some idea: to explain, justify, or hypothesize. To avoid any pitfalls, the teacher has to ask:

• Am I using wait-time before and after I receive responses to questions? (The wait-time allows students to think about their answers. Teachers with high expectations have a longer wait-time.)
• Am I exploring alternative strategies posed by different students? (How can I use student responses to promote classroom discussions? Can I promote student thinking by asking stretching questions?)

- Am I exploring unproductive thinking? (Depending on student answers, will I correct misconceptions so students do not have faulty thinking in their approach or will I use extension type questions that challenge student thinking? Can I guide the students back to productive thinking?)
- Am I using various forms of communication: reading, writing, listening, and speaking? (Remember, students process information through their senses so a multisensory approach will ensure that there is one sense that a student favors, that is, visual-auditory or tactile, so having information presented via all the senses will ensure that one sense is a student's preferred method.)
- Am I modeling scientific thinking? (Am I practicing oral rehearsal, elaborative interrogation, or self-regulation strategies? I must remember that self-regulation skills must be taught and modeled so the students will know how to do them when they are working independently.)
- What kind of questions are my students asking? (Based on the kinds of questions my students are asking, what information are they processing, what information needs to be clarified, expanded, or reinforced?)
- Are my students talking to each other—disagreeing, challenging, and debating? (How am I promoting discussions, probing thoughts, or challenging student thinking?)
- Are my students willing to take risks? (How can I encourage risk taking in my students, so they want to "think outside the box" when they are working on the assignment?)
- Are my students listening to each other? (Am I going to paraphrase, restate, or expand student answers to ensure that students are listening? Or, am I not going to paraphrase any answers to ensure that students are encouraged to listen?)
- Are my students taking time to think about the problem, question, idea, or the like? (Will I use a longer wait-time to give students time to think?)
- Are my students able to explain their ideas clearly and precisely? (Do I need to ask questions to expand student thinking to help students expand their ideas?)
- Are my *students able to reflect* on the experience and identify what was hard or easy for them, what worked and what didn't, what they liked and what they didn't? (Will I build in reflection in the process?)

SUMMARY

There are many pitfalls that teachers face when they develop or ask questions. The pitfalls vary and all have an impact on student learning. There are some common strategies that can be used, which can include:

1. Use questions to help students develop understanding.
2. Use questions to help decompose a problem.
3. Encourage student planning and self-regulation to solve problems.
4. Promote self-explanations, self-talk, and deep dives into the material.
5. Have students examine tier thinking to see if there are misunderstandings.
6. Have students understand the purpose.
7. Use stretching questions for brainstorming a topic, generating interest, and introducing topic-related vocabulary.
8. Use mind-mapping on the board, or in the form of a "what we know/what we would like to know/what we know now" framework.
9. Use a variety of questions which focus on form, function, meaning, concept, and strategies.

In the next chapter we will discuss strategies for instructional release.

REFERENCES

Albergaria-Almeida, P. (2010). Classroom questioning: Teacher's perceptions and practices. *Procedia Social and Behavioral Sciences*. Received October 5, 2009; revised December 14, 2009; accepted January 4, 2010. Retrieved from https://pdf .sciencedirectassets.com

Bennett, Colette. (2020). 7 ways teachers can improve their questioning technique. *ThoughtCo*, Feb. 11, 2020. Retrieved from thoughtco.com/ways-teachers-get-que stioning-wrong-8005.

Briggs, Saga. (2014). Socratic questioning: 30 thought-provoking questions to ask your students. *Blog*, November 8, 2014 taken from: Informed. Retrieved from www.opencolleges.edu.au/informed.

Brown, G. A., & Edmondson, R. (1985). Asking questions. In E. C. Wragg (ed.) *Classroom teaching skills* (pp. 97–120). London: Croom Helm.

Common Pitfalls of Questioning/Document. Retrieved from http://oer.educ.cam .ac.uk/w/index.php?title=Common_Pitfalls_of_Questioning/Document&oldid =8358

Corley, M. W., & Rauscher, C. (2013). *Deeper learning through questioning, TEAL Center Fact Sheet No. 12: Deeper Learning through questioning*. The Teaching Excellence in Adult Literacy (TEAL) Center is a project of the U.S. Department of Education, Office of Vocational and Adult Education (OVAE).

Dallimore, E., Hertenstein, J., & Platt, M. (2012). Impact of cold-calling on student voluntary participation. *Journal of Management Education, XX*(X), 1–37. DOI: 10.1177/1052562912446067

Dunlosky, J. (2013). *Strengthening the student toolbox*. American educator, Fall.

Effective Questioning, Educational Psychology Service, West Lothian civic Centre. Retrieved from http://www.westlothian.gov.uk/education/

Kelemanik, G., & Lucenta, A. (2019). Integrating effective teaching practices. *Ready Classroom Mathematics*. Retrieved from https://www.curriculumassociates.com/products/ready-classroom-mathematics/mathematics-effective-teaching-practices-whitepaper

Kerry, T. (2002). *Explaining and questioning*. London: Nelson Thornes.

Key Stage 3 National Strategy | Pedagogy and practice © Crown copyright 2004 Unit 7: Questioning DfES 0430-2004

National Governors Association Center for Best Practices, Council of Chief State School Officers. (2010). *Common core state standards initiative for mathematics*. Washington, DC: Author. Retrieved from http://www.corestandards.org/Math/

NCTM. (2014). *Principles to actions: Ensuring mathematical success for all*. Reston, VA: National Council of Teachers of Mathematics.

Pedagogy and practice: Teaching and learning in secondary schools" (ref: 0423-2004G) which can be downloaded from the National Archives http://webarchive.nationalarchives.gov.uk/20110809101133/nsonline.org.uk/node/97131

Roediger, H. L. III & Pyc, M. (2012). Inexpensive techniques to improve education: Applying cognitive psychology to enhance educational practice. *Journal of Applied Research in Memory and Cognition, 1*(4): 242–248.

Chapter 3

Instructional Release

TEXTBOX 3.1

What is the focus of this chapter?

This chapter will answer the question: What instructional delivery should I use?

Focus Questions:

1. What instructional delivery should I use?
2. What kinds of questions should I ask?
3. What kinds of questions should I use for whole-group and small-group questioning?

WHAT INSTRUCTIONAL DELIVERY SHOULD I USE?

When looking at the questioning process, the teacher should plan questions to use before, during, and after instruction because each phase of the instructional process requires a different type of question as each phase of instruction has a different purpose. The "before" phase is consistent with the Learner's Brain Model developed by Dr. Barbiere (2018) and involves the four stages: Planning, Readiness, Informational, and Closure. This is represented in figure 3.1.

One will notice that the bottom of the pyramid is "planning" as that phase will require the most time as a well-planned lesson requires multiple sources

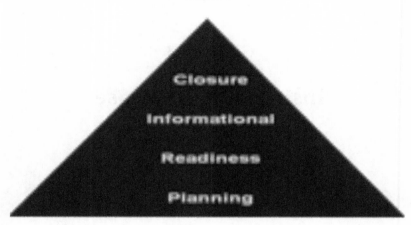

Figure 3.1   The Learner's Brain Model developed by Dr Barbiere

of data to use in order to be successful. Data from the lesson and data gathered at the end of the lesson are used to determine what worked and what needs to be revised based on "live" data from the lesson and student input at the end of the lesson. Considerations that the teacher must use are included in table 3.2.:

Before Instruction

How the learning domain is established for the scholars so they can function effectively in a safe, emotional environment is the first question that needs to be addressed in the teacher's planning. This is in essence the climate and

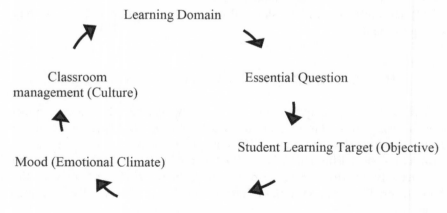

Figure 3.2   The Planning State of the Learner's Brain Model

culture that a teacher has established for her classroom. Questions teachers should consider during this planning stage are:

1. Do my students like my class? How will I know?
2. Are my students successful in my class? How will I know they are successful? Will I use a Demonstration of Student Learning (DSL) that addresses more than one intelligence for the student assessment?
3. What opportunities will I provide for my students to be successful?
4. What opportunities will I provide for students who are experiencing difficulties?
5. How will I set the tone in my classroom?
6. How will I reinforce the classroom climate and culture?
7. What self-regulation strategies will I build into the lesson? Will I provide the seeds for self-regulation starting with the Student Learning Target (Objective)?
8. How will I make sense and meaning of the lesson?
9. Will I incorporate overt and covert consolidation for closure in the lesson?

After the teacher has collected multiple sources of data to use for the lesson planning, she can begin her planning with the development of the Essential Question.

"Brain Break: The Essential Question is a thought-provoking statement that normally requires higher levels of cognition to answer, sparks further investigations, and represents the 'big picture' or grand scheme of things for the student. It cannot be answered by a yes or no. It helps the learner's brain see 'completeness' and the interrelationship of the short-term Student Learning Targets (SLT) to the big picture. It answers the student's question: 'why are we studying this?' because the short-term target is connected to it. The Student Learning Target is a pathway to the finished or desired goal."

"If the question leads to a more general point, then the intent trumps the type of question posed. Why you ask a question (in terms of seeking a desired result from asking it) matters more than how you phrase it. No question is inherently essential or trivial. Whether it is essential depends on purpose, audience, context, and impact. What do you as a teacher intend for students to do with the question? Hence a deep question dealing with concepts and understanding promotes a broader base of learning."

Once the Essential Question is developed, the teacher will plan the Student Learning Target (SLT).

"Brain Break: The Student Learning Target (SLT) is written using 'I statements' so the learner takes ownership, answers the question of what the student is expected to do, and, depending on the verb, it promotes an action which will be able to be measured, and relate to a desired outcome, that is, I will be able to write a research paper on the economic impact of the civil war citing five sources as opposed to: I will read five sources about the economic impact of the civil war. The critical point is to write an 'I statement' so the reader takes ownership. The adage is that people don't wash a rented car, so we want our learners to take ownership."

To help the teacher plan the SLT, the teacher should remember that the noun addresses the knowledge sought and the verb promotes the cognition. Table 3.1 serves as an example.:

Once the Student Learning Target is established, the teacher can determine what questions will be needed to help the students accomplish the task. Remember, for this phase of the planning, teacher questions are planned:

1. Promote student interest by tying in their prior knowledge. Remember it does not take much to activate prior knowledge. A simple question should suffice: Do you remember what we talked about yesterday?
2. What prompts, cues, or reinforcers will I plan to motivate the students?
3. What questions will I ask the class to encourage creativity and brainstorming: "Can you think about all the causes of the problem? Don't limit your thinking."
4. To focus attention on a specific problem: "Make a statement and compare the evidence from two texts you read to support your claim."
5. What clarifying questions will I plan to challenge student thinking? Is that always the case? What are other possibilities that can be considered?
6. What questions will I use to prompt students about alternate viewpoints? What is another consideration or possibility?
7. Will I ask students to consider the implications of their statements?

Table 3.1   Planning the Student Learning Target

STL: I will be able to write a research paper on the economic impact of the civil war citing five sources	
Verb: Although the task calls for writing, students will have to do research on the topic, analyze the data, synthesize the data, and then formulate an opinion for their research paper. Write	Noun: Research paper The student will have to have a minimum of five sources for their paper.
Alternatives: Construct a graph showing the economic impact of the war.	Alternate: I will develop a quiz to give to my classmates based on the five readings. (All students will read the same five articles.)
Reflection: Next time I will . . .	Reflection: I learned?

"Brain Break: The goal of a Readiness Set is to activate the student's prior knowledge, so the new information will be linked to existing knowledge. Without a link, the information is an 'orphan' and stays in short-term memory for 20–30 seconds and then is dismissed. The activation of prior knowledge connects the old and new to form a neural network. The more the neural network is used, the faster it becomes as the connection becomes myelinated. Hence, the adage 'practices slowly to get fast.' The slow practice develops neural networks and eventually the speed follows. The teacher will activate student's prior knowledge, by asking the class if they have seen a movie. The Readiness Set does not have to be long, but it does have to be meaningful. Asking the class if they saw a movie engages various parts of their brain, so the brain becomes receptive to new information. The teacher will say: 'today we are going to learn about movies and we will be working together to make our own mini movie.'"

Demonstration of Student Learning (DSL): The DSL is an assessment that is used to determine what was taught. In some cases, multiple intelligences can be used by students for the assessment. Although demonstrations of learning can vary widely in structure, purpose, evaluation criteria, and student learning objectives from school to school, they commonly require students to present, perform, explain, or defend their project design, theory or action, or results. Whether students solve a math problem, write a paper, design a project, or produce a work of art, drama, or engineering, demonstrations of learning require them to sow (demonstrate) their ideas. How will students show you they understand the concept being taught? The DSL is the answer.

"Brain Break: The DSL helps the brain 'see' completeness as the Student Learning Target (objective) which is the starting point of the lesson and the DSL which is the ending point. The SLT and the DSL are like bookends that bracket instruction. They are needed because they begin the first stage of self-regulation which is 'foreknowledge.' Students have to know what they will be studying and how they will be assessed so they know what they have to learn or research during the lesson. Students knowing how they will be assessed after the lesson is equally as important so they can plan their research to ensure they can address the assessment. Having a rubric to go with the assessment will enable the student to self-monitor and self-regulate their behavior and assess their progress. The advantage of a rubric is that it lowers barriers as students know what they need to do for each level, hence the ability to self-monitor and modulate their action."

Once the Essential Question, SLT, and DSL have been established, the emotional climate and culture of the classroom have to be planned. How will the emotional tone be set for the class? One way is to have well-established classroom procedures. For example:

Table 3.2   Using Multiple Intelligences to develop a DSL

SLT: I will be able to write a research paper on the economic impact of the civil war citing five sources DSL: I will be able to:	
Linguistic intelligence: Write a research paper using APA style of writing.	*Logical-mathematical*: Show the economic impact of the civil war using charts and graphs.
Interpersonal: Describe the economic impact as a descriptive discussion between two economists. I will work with another student to develop the dialogue.	*Intrapersonal*: Describe how the economic impact of the civil war affected me and my family. I will use a first-person narrative to tell my story
Reflection: I learned that . . .	Reflection: Next time I will . . .

1. Arrive to class on time.
2. Enter the classroom and be ready for instruction.
3. Be prepared for the daily assignment.
4. Check the whiteboard for the Essential Question, SLT, and DSL to start the process of self-regulation.
5. Be respectful in deeds and words.
6. Share the mike- one voice at a time.
7. Participate, learn, and enjoy.

These simple rules establish a protocol for students upon entering class. The more the teacher reinforces these rules, the easier her classroom management becomes as students know what to do when they enter the classroom. It also provides direction for the student after she enters the room. By focusing the student's attention to the SLT on the whiteboard, that action will trigger the student's attention to what they will be learning for the day. It is akin to the teacher telling the student to "pay attention."

As teachers, we know what it is like when students do not see the need in what they are studying or if what they are studying does not make sense. We get asked the "killer question: Is this going to be on the test?" or "Why do we have to know this?" With both questions, the student is telling the teacher something. The minute the teacher tells the student that the information will be on the test, the student will focus her attention. Posting the SLT and the DSL will also help to focus the student's attention.

Before instruction, the teacher will need to decide the following considerations:

1. The kinds of assessment that will be used so questions can be asked that support the assessment. For example, if the teacher will be using a

multiple-choice quiz, then her questions can be factual or comprehensive (Revised Bloom's Taxonomy lower level). Students will study differently for a multiple-choice quiz than an essay type quiz. A multiple-choice quiz requires memorization of facts and details while an essay quiz will require knowing concepts and deep understandings.

2. What cues or prompts will be provided during the lesson will indicate to the student what material is considered important, especially if the students are taking notes. When the students review their notes, they will see what the teacher emphasized in her review. For example, asking the student: "Can you justify your answer?" "Why do you feel that way?" and "Can you give me examples?" These are examples of cues that can be used to expand student thinking to get them ready for an essay type examination

3. How will I challenge students about assumptions: for example, "Do you think that this is always the case?", "Why do you think the author's assumption is accurate is a respectful way to engage a student in dialogue.

4. How can I provoke classroom discussion to get more student engagement and to create discussion? "Who agrees with Sandellie and why?" and "Who has a different point of view which they would like to share?"

5. How will I allow for alternative viewpoints and perspectives: for example, "What is the counter argument for?" "Can/did anyone see this in another way" (so as to foster more robust discussions)?

6. What questions am I planning to provoke student thinking about implications and consequences: for example, "But if what happened, what else would result?", "How does . . . affect . . . ?"

7. Will I build in time for students to question the question or challenge student comments? Will I do it via gallery walks, teams that support the plan (pro) and teams that don't support the plan (con). On the line is a group activity as well as four corners used by teachers.

Now that we have the student's attention, the next phase of the Learner's Brain Model is Instructional Delivery. In the Instructional Delivery phase, a process called "Gradual Release (GRR)" is used and it has three stages. The Instructional Delivery plan involves developing activities using a Gradual Release protocol.

Instructional Delivery plan is to do a GRR.

"Brain Break: The teacher will plan the lesson using the three-stage model of Gradual Release of Responsibility (GRR). There are three stages for GRR. The first stage is the teacher mode or the 'I do' model. The teacher may model the desired behavior or use oral rehearsal to explain a process to the students. Since most learners are visual learners, having the teacher model the behavior and explain the process will 'imprint' the process in the student's brain, and more importantly, it will be shown correctly."

"The second phase is the 'We do.' The teacher's role changes to a guide or facilitator using prompts, cues, or noticing providing additional modeling and demonstrations when needed. The teacher may find it necessary to model a particular strategy again, using some students' comments or understanding to demonstrate how to use the strategy effectively. This process will correct any misinformation or incorrect processes so the brain can process the correct procedure and develop neural networks that are 'correct.'"

"Finally, in the third stage, 'You do' students assume the responsibility for using the strategy in practice. They will have seen it done, practiced it and now apply it (Webb et al., 2019)."

"With the increasing demands of accountability, including No Child Left Behind (NCLB), Every Student Succeed Act (ESSA) Response to Intervention (RtI), Common Core State Standards (CCSS) (National Governors Association Center for Best Practices, Council of Chief State School Officers and most, if not all teacher evaluation models, encourages a gradual release protocol that provides opportunities for students to be engaged and asking questions. In essence, higher teacher rating for their evaluations occurs when the students are doing most of the work and not the teacher."

Gradual Release: "I Do" Stage

This phase is identified as the teacher provides direct instruction during this phase. This phase is very important as there is a lot of research on the importance of questioning. The research on teaching and learning strategy is well documented (Almeida et al., 2008; Chin & Osborne, 2008; Graesser & Olde, 2003). More importantly, it is suggested that teachers spend up to 50 percent of class time on questioning and that they ask between 300 and 400 questions a day (Levin & Long, 1981), while each student asks, on average, 1 question per week (Graesser & Person, 1994). Think about it for a minute, teachers are asking several hundred questions.

What was even more interesting was that teachers were not aware about their questioning patterns. How can one determine the kinds and amount of questions that a teacher asks during a lesson? The author developed a chart for questioning which is listed below.

The form above captures the teacher's question during a lesson and the kinds of questions a teacher asks. When shown the form they are usually surprised with the results.

The first column captures the teacher's activity. In the next column is the RBT category.

When a teacher asks a question, the question is identified in the Model Question category and it is then entered in the chart above by category. So, for example, teacher 1 asks a "what" question. Number one would be written

Table 3.3 Revised Bloom's Tananomy checklist

Knowledge Dimension	Factual Knowledge Basic elements to know	Tally Total	Conceptual Comprehension	Tally Total	Procedural: How to do something involves Analysis/Evaluation	Tally Total	Metacognition Create	Tally Total	Row Total
Create	Assemble, elaborate		Generate, produce, propose.		Design, devise, how would you test?,		Create, compose, improve.		
Evaluate	Judge, appraise, deduce.		Predict, critique, prioritize, argue.		Justify, verify, debate, evaluate.		Reflect, rationalize, prove.		
Analyze	Infer, distinguish, compare, contrast.		Compose, organize, categorize, analyze.		Illustrate, cause/effect, differentiate.		Deconstruct, attribute, make a chart.		
Apply	Show explain, build, organize.		Solve, produce.		Extend, apply, generalize, solve.		Use, implement.		
Understand	Demonstrate, explain, give examples, match, paraphrase.		Classify, interpret, distinguish.		Recognize, show, summarize.		Conclude.		
Remember	Recall, match Choose, find, label, name.		Locate info, recall, recite, show, find.		Describe.		Identify, from a list.		
Total Questions Captured:									

Teacher Directed   Student Directed

Source: Bloom (1954, 1956) revised by Anderson and Krathwohl (2001), examples from Dalton & Smith (1986) and Kuzmich (2011).

Table 3.4 Teacher Checklist of verbs to use, strategies to employ and model questions to ask

Teacher Activity: lecture, Review, etc.	RBT Category	Verbs	Instructional Strategies	Model questions
	Remember.	Choose, describe, find, identify, label, list, name, recall, recite, recognize.	Highlighting, memorizing, making a list, making a chart.	Who?, Where?, What?, How?, When?, What does it mean?
	Understand.	Demonstrate, distinguish, explain, give examples, match, paraphrase, show, summarize.	Students explain, state a rule, paraphrase, visual representation.	Statement on words. What does it mean? Give an example. Explain what is happening. What is the main idea? Is this the same as—? What are they saying? What seems likely?
	Apply	Apply, explain, generalize, judge, organize, produce, show, sketch, solve, use.	Apply in the real-world, case study, construct a model, explain an idea.	Predict what would happen? Tell me how, when, where, and why. Identify the results of—?, What is the function of—? Choose the best statements that apply.
	Analyze	Analyze, categorize, cause/effect compare, contrast, differentiated.	Jig-saw activity, What are the assumptions, relationships, and Instructional strategies to use.	Is that fact or opinion? What are the assumptions? What does the author believe? What is the relationship between the two points of view?, or pattern? What is the motive?
	Evaluate	Appraise, argue, estimate, criticize, debate, justify, verify.	Justify, prioritize, and rationalize, debate, evaluate.	Invalid?, Judge the effects, find errors, defend your point of view, justify your answer, isn't bias, fair, or ethical?
	Create	Compose, construct, design, devise, predict.	Design, create, devise, or compose.	How would you test, developing creative solution, invent a new system, process, procedure?

over what. Then Number 1 would be added to the remember category. This would continue for all the questions that the teacher asks.

If one then goes to visit another teacher, the "stroke counting" begins for that teacher. If teacher 2 asks a "what" question, then a 2 would be placed over what in the above chart and a 2 would be placed in the remember category. Below is the form completed:

As you can see, fifty-five of the seventy-five questions that were asked were low level or remember type of questions while three of the seventy-five were evaluate types of questions and five were analyze type. It was an eye-opening experience for the administrator and the teacher!

Questioning rubric: effective instruction/student communication

...edge Dimension	Factual Knowledge Basic elements to know	Conceptual Comprehension	Procedural: How to do a it Analysis Evaluation	Metacognition Create
Create	Assemble, elaborate,	Generate, produce, propose	Design, devise, how would you test ...	Create, compose, improve
Evaluate	Judge, appraise, deduce,	Predict, critique, prioritize, argue	Justify, verify, debate, evaluate,	Reflect, rationalize/prove 3/75
Analyze	Infer, distinguish compare, contrast	Compose, organize, categorize, analyze	Illustrate, cause/effect, differentiate 333	Deconstruct, attribute, make a chart 5/75
Apply	Show explain, build, organize,. 333	Solve, produce	Extend, apply, generalize, solve 33	Use, implement 5/75
Understand	Demonstrate, explain, give examples, match, paraphrase,	Classify, interpret distinguish	Recognize, show, summarize.	conclude 7/75
Remember	Repeat, match Choose, find, label, name,	locate info, recall, recite, show, find	Describe .	Identify, from a list 55/75

Source: Bloom (1954 and 1956) revised by Anderson and Krathwohl (2001) examples from Dalton, and Smith (1986) and Kuzmich (2011)

Teacher Activity: lecture, review, etc.	RBT Category	Verbs	Instructional Strategies	Model questions
	Remember	Choose, describe, find, identify, label, list, name, recite, recognize.	highlighting, memorizing, make a list, make a chart.	What?, Who?, Why?, How?, When?, What does it mean?
	Understand	Demonstrate, distinguish explain, give examples, match, paraphrase, show, summarize.	students explain, state a rule, paraphrase, visual representation	Statement on words. What does it mean? . Give an example. , Explain what is happening, What is the main idea? Is this the same as....? What are they saying? What seems likely?
	Apply	Apply, explain, generalize, judge, organize, produce, sketch, solve, use,	Apply in the real world, case study, construct a model, explain an idea	Predict what would happen, Tell me how, when, where and why?, Identify the results of...?, What is the function of...? Choose the best statements that apply...
	Analyze	Analyze, categorize, cause/effect compare, contrast, differentiated	Jigsaw activity, What are the assumptions, relationship and	Is that fact or opinion, What are the assumptions? What does the author believe?, What is the relationship between..?, State a point of view, or pattern?, What is the motive?
	Evaluate	appraise, argue, estimate, criticize, debate, justify, verify	justify, prioritize and rationalize, debate, evaluate	invalid?, Judge the effects, finding errors, defend your point of view, justify your answer, isn't bias, fair or ethical?
	Create	compose, construct, design, device predict	Design, create, devise or compose	how would you test, developing creative solution invent a new system, process, procedure

© M. Barbiere Ed.D, February 2013

Figure 3.3   Form uses to plot teacher questions

During Instruction: "I Do" Stage Continued

In the Danielson Model, a distinguished rating for Element 1, Setting Instructional Outcomes, the teacher encourages her students to set their own goals; she provides them a taxonomy of challenge verbs to help them strive to meet the teacher's higher expectations of them (Danielson, 2013). Providing challenge verbs is also important in McREL Teacher Evaluation Systems, Element d, teachers help students understand new knowledge by using curs, questions, and advanced organizers. The effective use of this strategy includes focusing on what is important, using explicit curs, asking inferential questions, and asking analytic questions.

In all cases, talk mediates learning, so the task is to have students talk and the higher-level questions promote discussion especially when it is done with an open-ended question.

During the "I do" phase, the key to the planning of questions is for the teacher to know that this phase of instruction is "direct instruction" by the teacher. Hence, the teacher questioning should be focused on promoting student interest, providing information to the student as they will be able to work independently. This may mean asking factual kinds of questions to ensure that students have enough background knowledge on the topic. Or, it may mean asking more analytic questions.

It is interesting to note the role of questioning as thinking is not driven by answers but mostly by questions as the questions promote thinking while the

Table 3.5 Questions and Instructional strategies for using a Gradual Release of Responsibility plan (GRR)

Process	Guiding Question	Instructional practice
I do—direct instruction	• What assessment am I planning? How will that guide my questioning? • How will I scaffold my questions to ensure that students will be able to do the assignment?	• Readiness Set • Factual information • Application questions • Check for understanding • To monitor progress • 20 minutes for instruction
We do	• After I model the behavior, what questions will I plan to motivate the students? • What questions will I ask to check for student understanding? • How will I "release" the students for the next phase?	• Modeling behavior • Oral rehearsal. • Multiple step problems to show the process. • Pair-sharing. • Check for Understanding.
I do	• How will I provide feedback to the students? • What questions will I use to promote understanding? • How will I assess students?	• Using higher-level types of questions to promote cognition • Covert closure • Overt closure

answers are the outcome of the thinking. More importantly, the perception is that students who usually ask questions in the classroom tend to learn and think better than those who are quiet during most of the class time. On the importance of questioning in the classroom, effective questions, that is, those that promote analysis, evaluation, and synthesis, can therefore lead to deeper student understandings as students are processing the information, interpreting it, and coming to conclusions.

During the instructional phase, the teacher will be promoting student thinking by doing checks for understanding beginning with questions that promote factual knowledge then moving to questions that promote analysis and evaluation.

"Brain Break: Checks for understandings are strategies that the teacher uses throughout the lesson to provide feedback to the student; feedback is valuable information to the teacher so he or she can assess how students are doing and then make any necessary adjustments to the lesson. The goal is to ensure that correct information is processed during the lesson so when the students practice, they will use 'perfect practice' or only use the appropriate skills to master the task. Practice does not make perfect. If a student practices a skill incorrectly, they will have practiced the skill and learned it but it was practiced and learned incorrectly. The brain will have developed an incorrect neural network which will be difficult to unlearn. Hence the adage that perfect practice makes perfect. In essence, the brain forms neural networks from the practice and the more one practices, the neural network becomes myelinated and the action is done more quickly. Practice, practice, practice, and it leads to speed."

WHOLE-GROUP AND SMALL-GROUP PLANS

TEXTBOX 3.2

With whole-class instruction. The teachers should:

- Reinforce class expectations, that is, cold calling, range of questions planned.
- Tell the class that there will three phases during the lesson.
- Tell the class that there will be wait-time after questions.
- Consolidation for closure will be done at the end of the lesson.

Clarify Concepts. These are questions that are clarifying what was stated and should not express an opinion or bias. It has to be a simple request for additional information (mostly factual). Hence: "Do you mean?" "Can you please clarify that comment?" Can you give me a little more information on what you mean? The goal is for the teacher to assess how deeply the student has thought about the subject.

Probing Questions: These are useful after the topic has been introduced so students have a frame of reference and understanding to the topic. The questions can be asked after a homework assignment or after a class lesson. The teacher can use the Readiness Set as a pre-readiness or provide a reading assignment for homework. The teacher can use the reading assignment as one way to introduce information which will be covered. This is necessary as the teacher can't ask probing questions unless the students have knowledge and have formed an opinion on the topic. The teacher can ask the students to share any struggles in the story and what conclusions they reached: those of you who reached the conclusion x, have you considered y? Additional questions: "Can you convince the rest of the class about you answer?" "Tell me how that makes sense?" "Did anyone revise their assumptions after hearing the answer?" "Is there a different way of saying the same thing?" "Really? Are you sure? Is there another explanation?"

Probing questions to test a rationale, reasons, and evidence. "How did you come to that conclusion?" "Can you share what method you used to solve the problem?" "What is another way to solve this math problem?" "How can you prove your answer?"

Another variation of a probing question is a question to test a student's viewpoints and perspectives. For example, "Who agrees with Rahim and why?" "How were you sure you had the correct answer?"

Probing Implications and Consequences: It is another version of probing questions whereby you are asking a question to challenge the students thinking to get them to think differently, that is, "What is another way to think about the answer?" "If you did this, what would happen?" "What assumptions did you make to solve this problem?" (For math classes, the teacher can ask: "Can you draw a picture or make a model to prove your answer?")

The probing questions can work in a large group or in a small group. Let's explore small group.

Small-Group Questioning: How Do We Do It?

There are several ways to go from large group discussions to small group discussions. Below are a few of the ways and possible questions to ask.

Circle Discussion: After the large-group discussion, the teacher can have the group separate into two small groups and sit in a circle. The circle arrangement can be done right after the large-group activity to allow for more students to partake in discussion or at the end of the small-group activity to serve as an "evaluation discussion." In this scenario, the teacher will summarize student responses to help them make connections:

1. Lisette said x, how many people felt the same? Did anyone feel differently? The question can be used to determine how the students feel about a topic and to assess how many share the same opinion.
2. What stands out from your research?
3. What conclusions did you arrive at during your reading?

Reteach Group: During the course of instruction, the teacher will notice that some students are not doing well, or during her checks for understandings, she sees that students need extra help. Having a small group arrangement can aid in re-teaching the concept. During the instructional period, the teacher questioning will assess student knowledge.

Pre-teach Group: Teachers can group students based on skill level into a small group to provide an opportunity for pre-teaching specific vocabulary, challenging text structures, or other prerequisite knowledge to English Language Learners, students with Special needs, or students who require additional support. This will prepare the students for the lesson they will be receiving. In. this model, the teacher has to prepare factual questions for the students because she is developing their knowledge base. The factual questions will help make sense of the lesson.

Jig-saw: The teacher will develop small groups and assign each person in the group a section to read and become an expert on what they have read. The philosophical approach is for each group to develop expertise on its particular subtopic by brainstorming, developing ideas, and researching the topic. They will also be required to report out to the class. Jig-sawing requires students to listen and learn, and the group is rewarded when each individual contributes their skills and knowledge to the whole.

Not only is learning improved but tolerance and understanding are improved as well. When planning a jig-saw activity, provide a list of questions to the students so they can be focused when they have their discussion: "What was the author's intent?", "How can this be applied today?", "How does what you read make sense?", "How does what you read fit into the big picture?" Remember: you will be teaching the rest of the class what you read so pick out the important details of your section.

An alternative approach is that once students have become experts on a particular subtopic, shuffle the groups so that the members of each new group have a different area of expertise. Or, have each member report out what they found in their group to discuss with the new group to see if there was a different point of view on the subject. By having students taking turns and sharing their expertise with the other group members they are putting the "puzzle" (the topic researched) together.

One potential drawback is that students hear only one group's expertise on a particular topic and don't benefit as much from the insight of the whole class. To counter this drawback, the teacher has to address the whole group during the report out to do a check for understanding to see who had a different idea. Or, the teacher can keep a written record of each group's work and create a master document—a completed puzzle—on the topic to share out with the students.

Me and My Friends: The teacher constructs a small group of students. They are given an assessment to complete as a group. Tasks are assigned to groups with the understanding that they have to explore more than one answer or way to solve a problem and then share what they found with the entire group. The group will decide what the best answer is to the question. The task is to develop collaboration skills, listening skills, research skills, and problem-solving skills. This activity lends itself to a variety of possibilities like developing dialogue for a historical event, writing a script for a television dramatization or show, developing a fictional or futuristic event, or running a country or government during a crisis. An alternate plan is to have the students do the work of planning what to do and assignment of subtasks.

I Go, You Go: This strategy involves students discussing issues with many of their fellow classmates in a specific order. The student's grouping can be any number and any arrangement, that is, arranged in a circle or square. As a pre-readiness activity for the students the teacher gives the group a question to answer. One starts and everyone listens to what was said but does not react. After everyone in the group has an opportunity to respond, they summarize their finding and report out. For example, if Ojas was reporting out, he would say: "I agree with Sandy's point as I reached the same conclusion. I disagree with Frank's assessment because . . . . In this manner he would have had to listen to all the students in the circle and analyzed what they said."

The activity can be used as a Readiness Set by asking students to read the passage and develop questions to ask the teacher. The development of questions by the students will promote their interest in the topic and developing questions will promote a deeper dive on their part as they seek meaning from what they are reading. As an assessment activity, you can provide the group with assessment questions they have to answer. The answer sheet could be used for the whole group or individual answers from each student. If the teacher used individual answers, that activity can be their exit ticket or a consolidation for closure activity as students will submit their answers to the teacher on the way out of the class. Another approach is for the teacher to pose a more complex question to the students to answer for the closure activity.

Snowball: This is a fun activity which will require time for the students to get to know how to use the process and to do it effectively. The task is to "grow the snowball" by adding to the original group to make it bigger. This method involves doubling the grouping of students until a desired number is reached. The teacher starts with developing pairs of students. The task is for the pairs to work collaboratively. The teacher can give the pairs a list of questions for them to answer. The students work cooperatively to find answers to the questions. For this grouping of students, the teacher will provide factual questions so as to ensure that the students are gathering background knowledge. After a period of time, the groups meet to share answers. After they share information, the teacher has to determine if the students have enough background knowledge to do the nest stage of the "snowball" which was analysis and synthesis.

So, when the group of two becomes a group of four, they will have factual information to begin the analysis, synthesis, and evaluation. The factual information is necessary to dig deeper in the material so the teacher will present higher-level questions to the students to promote metacognition. Working in a small group, the students can collaborate, test the hypothesis, and then draw conclusions. After they answer the questions, they will report out to the large groups so everyone can share their ideas.

By providing a sequence of increasingly complex tasks so that students do not become bored with repeated discussion at multiple stages, the teacher is scaffolding the skills array to bring the students to a higher metacognitive level.

An alternative approach is to have the students individually record their answers in their groups of two. When they report out, the teacher can do checks for understandings to see how many agree with the findings. They can then be placed into groups of four to first determine their findings and then to come to consensus as a group to report out their results.

In pairs, students try to answer one another's questions. Pairs join together to make fours and identify, depending on the topic, either unanswered questions or areas of controversy or relevant principles based on their previous discussions.

Fishbowl: This activity develops observation powers through group interaction. More importantly, the teacher can provide students questions to help develop analysis skills. This method involves one group observing another group. The first group forms a circle and either discusses an issue or topic, does a role play, or performs a brief drama. The second group forms a circle around the inner group. Depending on the inner group's task and the context of your course, the outer group can look for themes, patterns, soundness of argument, etc., in the inner group's discussion, analyze the inner group's functioning as a group, or simply watch and comment on the role play

Comments: As a teacher, be aware that the outer group members can become bored if their task is not challenging enough as they are just observing. So, the task is to develop questions to keep the students in the outer circle focused on the dialogue of the students in the inner circle.

The task is to ensure analytical questions are posed to the outer groups so they can assess the inner group's reasoning. Students in the outer circle can change places with the students in the inner circle to challenge their assumptions.

I have a question do you have the answer activity? Students develop questions after reading a passage. After they read the passage, they develop questions for their peers. With small groups developed, the teacher can monitor student action and provide frequent and individualized feedback to promote metacognition.

Phone a Friend (Build Confidence Through Collaboration): The teacher develops small groups and asks the students to develop questions for the other group. They will also have to have the answers to the questions they ask. If the other group cannot answer a question, they can phone a friend (the other group) if they cannot answer the question. The winning team can then develop questions to use for a subsequent quiz.

Questioning Students at the End of the Class

Teaching is mostly used by teachers because it is essential to know students' understanding, to assess students' learning, to test students' input, and to evaluate both a teacher's teaching quality and the teaching-learning process to determine whether they have been running well or not.

What Questions Should I Ask after Small Group Instruction?

At the end of a lesson, the critical factor for the teacher is having students talk. From theory, research, and anecdotal experience, we know talk mediates learning and having students talk, provides information to the teacher on what the students learned. Hence, closure is student talk. If the teacher does the talking, it is called review. The activity at the end of the lesson is called consolidation for closure. The information the students take home at the end of the lesson is very important as information is consolidation when they go to sleep. So, it is important that the information that is consolidated is accurate.

Consolidation for Closure: *Brain Break*: *Consolidation for Closure is important as it provides two important functions. One function is to take information from the daily lessons and consolidate the information when one sleeps. It is therefore important that the student's take away from the lesson is accurate because that is what will be consolidated at night. The second important function is to provide the teacher with information*

Hence, the rule of thumb is that closure is when the student talks. If the teacher talks, it is review. Knowing the importance of consolidation for closure, it is important that teachers set time aside at the end of the lesson to do this activity.

RECAP

Questioning is very powerful before, during, and after a lesson:

1. Being clear about how you will promote, measure, and celebrate understanding
2. Modeling *how to think* for students
3. Helping students understand what's worth understanding
4. Diversifying what you accept as evidence of understanding
5. Creating curriculum and instruction around a need to know
6. Collaborating with students to create the rubric or scoring guide
7. Letting students choose the project's purpose
8. Choosing "power standards" from your curriculum after meeting with students, parents, and community members that voice their unique societal and cultural needs
9. Letting students choose their own media form that reflects the purpose of the reading
10. Choice boards
11. Placing struggling readers in a lit circle, that gives them an authentic role that they can be successful in, allows them to hear oral fluency and reading speed model and keeps them from feeling "broken"
12. Starting class with a story
13. Using the on-demand writing prompt as the summative assessment
14. Framing learning in terms of process and growth and purpose
15. Choosing what's graded carefully and considering other work as practice

SUMMARY

Questions asked individually pertained to validation of common beliefs and misconceptions, basic information, explanations, and imagined scenarios. The findings regarding questions asked collaboratively are presented as two assertions. Assertion 1 maintained that students' course of learning was driven by their questions. Assertion 2 was that the ability to ask the "right" questions and the extent to which these could be answered were important in sustaining students' interest in the project. Above all, the goal is to promote student thinking and discussion

REFERENCES

Albergaria-Almeida, P. (2010). Classroom questioning: Teachers' perceptions and practices. *Procedia Social and Behavioral Sciences, 2*, 305–309.

Alexander, R. (2005). *Towards dialogic teaching*. York, UK: Dialogos.

Almeida, P., & Neri de Souza, F. (2009). Patterns of questioning in science classrooms. In M. Muñoz & F. Ferreira (eds.) *Proceedings of the IASK (International Association for the Scientific Knowledge) International Conference "Teaching and Learning 2009"* (pp. 125–132). Porto, Portugal, December 7–9.

Archer, A., & Hughes, C. (2010). *Explicit instruction: Effective and efficient teaching.* New York, NY: Guilford.

Barbiere, M. (2018). *Setting the stage: Delivering the plan using the learner's brain model*. Maryland: Rowman & Littlefield.

Barbiere, M. (2018). *Activating the learner's brain: Using the learner's brain model.* Maryland: Rowman & Littlefield.

Biddulph, F., Symington, D., & Osborne, R. (1986). The place of children's questions in primary science education. *Research in Science and Technological Education, 4*, 77–88.

Brookfield, S. D., & Preskill, S. (1999). *Discussion as a way of teaching: Tools and techniques for democratic classrooms.* San Francisco: Jossey-Bass Publishers.

Brualdi Timmins, Amy C. (1998). Classroom questions. Practical Assessment, Research, and Evaluation: Vol. 6, Article 6. DOI: https://doi.org/10.7275/05rc-jd18 Available at: https://scholarworks.umass.edu/pare/vol6/iss1/6

Chin, C., & Chia, L. G. (2004). Problem-based learning: Using students' questions to drive knowledge construction. *Science Education, 88*, 707–727.

Chin, C., & Osborne (March, 2008). J Student questions; a potential resource for teaching and learning science. *Studies in Science Education, 44*(1): 1–39.

Cotton, K. (2001). *Classroom questioning*. North West Regional Educational Laboratory.

Cox, S. & Griffith, A. (2007). *Outstanding teaching*. England: Crown House Publishing Limited.

Etemadzadeh, A., Seifi, S., & Roohbakhsh, H. (2013). The role of questioning technique in developing thinking skills; The ongoing effect on writing skill. *Procedia - Social and Behavioral Sciences, 70*, 1024–1031.

Fisher, R. (1990). *Teaching children to think*. London: Simon and Shuster.

Graesser, A., & Person, N. K. (1994). Question asking during tutoring. *American Educational Research Journal, 31*, 104–137.

Group Work in the Classroom: Types of Small Groups. Centre for Teaching Excellence, University of Waterloo.

Habeshaw, S., Habeshaw, T., & Gibbs, G. (1984). *53 interesting things to do in your seminars & tutorials*. Bristol: Technical and Educational Services Ltd.

Hollingsworth, J., & Ybarra, S. (2009). *Explicit direction instruction (EDI): The power of the well-crafted, well-taught lesson*. Thousand Oaks, CA: Corwin.

Johnson, D. W., Johnson, R. T., & Smith, K. A. (1991). *Cooperative learning: Increasing college faculty instructional productivity*. ASHE-ERIC Higher Education Report No.4. Washington, DC: School of Education and Human Development, George Washington University

Levin, T., & Long, R. (1981). *Effective instruction*. Washington, DC: Association for Supervision and Curriculum Development.

Millar, R., & Osborne, J. F. (Eds.) (1998). *Beyond 2000: Science education for the future*. London: King's College London.

Penick, J. E., Crow, L. W., & Bonnsteter, R. J. (1996). Questions are the answers. *Science Teacher, 63*, 26–29.

Rosenshine, B., Meister, C., & Chapman, S. (1996). Teaching students to generate questions: A review of the intervention studies. *Review of Educational Research, 66*, 181–221.

Silberman, M. (1996). *Active learning: 101 strategies to teach any subject*. Boston: Allyn and Bacon.

Slavin, R. E. (1995). *Cooperative learning: Theory, research, and practice*, 2nd ed. Boston: Allyn and Bacon.

Vygotsky, L. S. (1962, 1986). *Thought and language*. Cambridge, MA: MIT Press.

Vygotsky, L. S. (1978). *Mind in society: The development of higher psychological processes*. Cambridge, MA: Harvard University Press.

Webb, S., Massey, D., Goggans, M., & Flajole, K. (July/August, 2019). *Thirty-five years of the gradual release of responsibility: Scaffolding towards complex and responsive teaching* (pp. 95–83). Chicago, IL: University of chicago.

Chapter 4

Effective Questioning

TEXTBOX 4.1

What is the focus of this chapter?

This chapter will focus on determining effective questions and how to provide activities to determine question effectiveness.

Focus Questions:

1. What is an effective question?
2. When are the different types of questions necessary?
3. How can one determine if her questions are effective?

INTRODUCTION: WHAT WAS YOUR FAVORITE QUESTION?

Have you wondered why a question that you asked is a favorite question? Perhaps the question was something you were expecting or hoping to be asked so your anticipation of the question finally came? Specific questions are tailored for desired results. As teachers, we can plan our questions because we know the desired goal we are trying to achieve so our questions can bring a student to the level we are seeking. Let's look at types of questions and the desired result we are seeking.

The Role of Questioning in Instruction

Research on the question that teachers ask shows that about 60 percent require only recall of facts, 20 percent require students to think, and 20 percent are procedural in nature (Blosner, 1975). Researchers studying teachers' questioning patterns found that 53 percent of the questions that teachers asked stood alone and 47 percent were part of a sequence of two or more questions. Of this 47 percent, only 10 percent were a part of a sequence having four or more questions (Wragg & Brown, 2001). In short, teachers ask a preponderance of questions for students to retrieve factual information. Asking questions for factual information is important as it scaffolds to higher levels including metacognition.

Below is a breakdown of the types of questions using Revised Blooms Taxonomy (RBT) of Factual, Conceptual, Procedural, and Metacognitive levels and the purpose they serve.

Factual Questions

Example

Below is a transcript from a Saturday Night Live skit featuring Jerry Seinfeld on October 8, 2019 (retrieved at: https://www.theretrosite.com/jerry-seinfeld -history-class-on-saturday-night-live/). The cast was a list of who's featuring whom: Mr. Thompson: Jerry Seinfeld, Randy: Chris Farley, Sabrina: Ellen Clehorne, Lisa: Beth Cahill, Larry: Adam Sandler, Darlene: Melanie Hutsell, Doug: David Spade, Siobhan: Siobhan Fallon, and Chris: Chris Rock

The opening is the interior of a high school classroom with the teacher, Mr. Thompson, erasing a drawing from the chalkboard as his class enters.

Mr. Thompson*:* This is *not* funny. [bell rings] Alright, let's settle down, let's settle down. I've graded your tests, and I have to say, I am *more* than a little disappointed. In fact, I've decided I'm going to throw them all out. [pitches them] *The teacher is setting expectations that he thought the class would do better but feels that it was his instruction that was the problem. What can he do differently to ensure better student success? Some teachers would blame the students for not paying attention or not studying hard enough. This teacher is looking at himself as the problem that needs to be addressed.*
Randy: [arms in air] All-right!! [Mr. Thompson leers at him] I mean… aw, man.
Mr. Thompson: I think I've been placing too much emphasis on details. What I want you to do now is forget about memorizing things. I want you to *think* history, okay? We're just gonna make each other think. Okay? Now, is everybody

with me on this? *Note: Mr. Thompson is trying to get the class to move from facts to broad issues and concepts and to get to that point, he presents two events so students can see the relationship and draw conclusions. He states:* Alright, now let's talk about the Battle of Britain, and the Lend-Lease Act. How are these two events linked in history? Anybody got any thoughts? [a hand is raised] Sabrina?

Sabrina: So... the tests that you threw out, that's not gonna count? *(Student is off track and still thinking about test). He re-directs the student's attention by:*

Mr. Thompson: No. No. Everybody got that? Now, back to the Battle of Britain and the Lend-Lease Act. Roosevelt said that America must be the great arsenal of democracy. Now, what did he mean by that? We must be the great arsenal. What does he mean? Randy? *(Teacher is still trying to have the students see relationships)*

Randy: Uh... that we had to be.. this big.. arseno?

Mr. Thompson: Arsenal. With an "L."

Randy: Oh... right. That we needed to be... uh... I'm not sure I understand what you're asking.

Mr. Thompson: Okay. Maybe that wasn't a fair question. Alright. Now, what country did Roosevelt want to supply with weapons? Who can tell me? What country? Remember, we're talking about the Battle of.. *what*? Who can tell me? [a hand is raised] Lisa. *(Note: Teacher realizes that the students need more factual information before they can analyze and evaluate the two events he posed. So, he uses factual type questions of Who and What. He even tries to activate their prior knowledge by reminding the students that they talked about the Battle before today's lesson. The question is: were there checks for understanding during the lesson and a closure activity at the end? If not, then the assumption is that the students learned the lesson, which in this case, proved incorrect.*

Lisa: Uh.. Britain..?

Mr. Thompson: Yes! Good! You see, *now* we're thinking History!

Larry: [interrupting] Mr. Thompson? I was about to say Britain?

Mr. Thompson: That's good. So, Roosevelt wants to help Britain in the war against who? Who? Who is Britain at war with? Who can tell me? [no responses] Okay, let's think now. What was happening in America in the 1930's? [a hand is raised] Darlene. *(Note: the teacher continues to use factual questions to develop the student's knowledge)*

The attempt of the teacher was initially to have students see relationships and analyze facts. Unfortunately, the students lacked the factual information to get to that level so he revised his plan and asked lower-level questions to help them have a more extensive knowledge base. At this point of the lesson the use of questions to develop factual information was appropriate.

Table 4.1   Using Factual Questions as seen in Mr Thompson's lesson

Question Type: Factual	Purpose	Rationale
These types of questions are usually prefaced by who, what, when, where, and how types of questions.	Factual questions require a fact-based answer. Since there is a fact-based answer, there is usually a specific answer to the question. Since the factual questions have specific answers, the questions are usually short and do not require a long explanation. Hence, it is possible for teachers to ask a lot of factual questions that can be posed.	Teachers use factual questions to assess student knowledge. Once the teacher knows the students' level of factual knowledge, he or she can determine if they have enough factual knowledge to be able to analyze data. For English Language Arts, the teacher will ask factual questions and have students refer to the text to support their answers.
How many students agree with x?	Check for understanding used to assess student knowledge.	Checks for understanding are used to assess what students know so the teacher can monitor and adjust the lesson.

The attempt of Mr. Thompson was to talk about the "big picture" as he told the class: "I think I've been placing too much emphasis on details. What I want you to do now is forget about memorizing things. I want you to think history, okay?" So, let's see what kind of questions he can ask to promote concepts and the big picture (see table 4.1).

USING FERMI QUESTIONS

One approach to move to the next level is to use Fermi Questions. The purpose of the Fermi Question is to promote student thinking of big concepts. The Fermi question provides limited information, so students look to understand and test big ideas to drill down to their answer. The goal is to determine an order-of-magnitude answer by having the student make reasonable assumptions about the situation, not necessarily relying on definite knowledge for an exact answer but more of developing and understanding or path to resolve the problem.

A "Fermi Question" asks for a quick estimate of a quantity that initially seems difficult or impossible to determine precisely. Fermi's approach to questions relies on the use common sense and rough estimates of quantities pieced together a ball-park value. One example of a Fermi Question is:

(Fermi Questions, retrieved at: http://www.math.lsa.umich.edu/WCMTC/
Fermi-Questions-RCMC-Three-Levels.pdf): "What is an estimate of the
number of piano tuners in Chicago?" An approach to this problem is to break
the process into steps: estimate the population, estimate the number of households in the population, estimate the fraction of households that have pianos,
estimate how often each household has its piano tuned, estimate the time it
takes to tune a piano, estimate how many hours a piano tuner would work
each week, and so on. In this case, it is possible to check the estimate by looking in the phone book to see how many piano tuners are actually in Chicago.

Before the students work on the problem, they can brainstorm or list key
questions that need to be considered in finding a solution. A list of questions
can be developed and identified as being essential for solving this question.

The goal of the questioning is to promote thinking for conceptual understandings and apply that thinking to real-life problems for a resolution of a
problem. The questions serve to lead the students to an estimation which will
help them frame their answer. How close was I to the answer and what did I
do that I could have done differently?

Mr. Thompson could ask the class a variety of questions.

Conceptual

There are sample questions which include:

1. What's the purpose for the Lend Lease Act?
2. Please make a t-chart to compare your data.
3. After you make your chart, please share your information with your
   tablemate.
4. Summarize your information as you will be called upon to share your
   thinking on how you reached your conclusion.
5. What evidence or data was needed to understand the Battle of Britain and
   the Lend Lease Act?
6. Collect as many facts as you can about the Battle of Britain and the Lend
   Lease Act as you will be asked to develop a T-chart and you will be asked
   to justify your conclusions.
7. Why should the United States loan money or material to countries at
   war?

Procedural

There are different types of knowledge, so we move from factual (knowledge
of facts) to conceptual (connecting the facts into concepts knowledge). Once

Table 4.2   Using Questions to Develop Conceptual Knowledge

Questions: Concepts (Conceptual Knowledge)	Purpose	Rationale
Analyze.	Questions are used to promote a conceptual understanding of the topic by helping the students break down information from facts to broad concepts. The ability to take facts (horizontal information) and weave them together into deeper concepts (vertical information) is important, It is the tying together of information from isolated bits to form a broad-based concept.	In order to understand concepts and the big picture, students need to know facts and have information. Asking students to analyze information so they can determine critical facts and data to use to draw conclusions. How and Why questions that ask students to justify their reasoning will also be helpful in provoking thought.
Compare and contrast types Justify your answer.	Analysis of critical facts.	Students take individual or isolated facts and weave them together into concepts. They will broaden their understanding as the information/facts are being applied to broader concepts.

concepts are understood, the next step is to apply the concepts. The application process helps to reinforce the concepts until the process becomes second nature.

For example, you can score 100 percent in your driving theory test. You can study the owner's manual and know exactly what the law is or the rules of the road. Studying for a test and knowing answers is necessary to pass the test but there is also a road test that is required. Taking a test is different than driving a car. Who can forget the process of parallel parking? In this case, declarative knowledge of driving is useful to know what to do when you are on the road but not useful for actually driving a car. Procedural knowledge is developed when one practices driving the car itself. Having that example in mind, the teacher must provide activities and tasks that allow students to practice what they are learning.

Metacognition

Here's one way you can design effective questions:

Table 4.3 Developing questions to promote Procedural Knowledge

Questions: Process (Procedural Knowledge)	Purpose	Rationale
Justify, evaluate, and find.	Different from declarative knowledge, which is explicit, procedural knowledge is performed by doing as opposed to telling.	To promote metacognition, the student has to take facts and apply the facts.
How?	Procedural knowledge differs from declarative knowledge. Procedural knowledge is knowledge which can be demonstrated.	Develop reasoning, problem solving, and critical thinking. The application of the concepts becomes second nature or automated.
Can you give me an example? Can you show, paraphrase, summarize, distinguish, or demonstrate x?	The student demonstrates or applies concepts to show his or her understanding.	Asking open-ended questions promotes discussion. Closed questions require a yes or no answer and not demonstration on understanding. To promote understanding, the teacher asks students to show, summarize, or paraphrase to encourage student cognition so the student can apply the knowledge.
"What would happen if ..." questions.	Have students make predictions, estimations, or hypotheses and design ways to test them. The student has to have an understanding of concepts so they can apply the concepts in a practical way.	Engage students to challenge assumptions, share ideas, think outside the box to help them think of ways to apply the concepts.

Table 4.4 Questioning for developing Metacognition

Questions: Product (Metacognition for Creation)	Purpose	Rationale
Ask questions that allow learners to reflect on their own learning processes and strategies. Have them practice "oral rehearsal" and share their thinking.	To take information, have students practice oral rehearsal to share their thinking.	Promote student self-regulation. Metacognitive skills are more effective when tied to a specific content.

THE THINKING PROCESS FOR QUESTIONS

Readiness Stage

The goal of this stage is to tie students' frame of reference to the new material. In the Mr. Thompson scenario, the lesson was about the Battle of Britain and the Lend Lease Act. When developing questions for this stage the main goal is to hook students' interest.

1. Will this question promote students' frame of reference?
2. Can I use something in the school that students can relate to as a frame of reference Does this question draw out and work with pre-existing understandings that students bring with them?
3. Does this question raise the visibility of the key concepts the students are learning?
4. Will students see the relationship between their experiences and what they are learning so as to make the information meaningful and sensible?

Instructional Delivery Stage

Once the students' interests are stimulated, instruction is delivered. Let's look at questions for the various types of delivery. For large-group instruction, the teacher provides direct instruction and information, so the focus is twofold: to ask questions to develop factual knowledge and to spark their interest when they work in small groups. Below is a list of questions that can be posed which will cause students to seek information and which will be useful to gain facts and analyze the facts to make inferences.

1. What was the main goal Hitler wanted to accomplish by bombing the British air force in the Battle of Britain?
2. What new technology helped the British air force in defending against the Germans?
3. How did the British address the fact that the German air force, Luftwaffe, was larger in number than the British air force, the Royal Air Force?
4. What was Operation Sealion?
5. What is the Dowding System?
6. Who were the few?
7. What was the Blitz?

The purpose of these questions is to use them as a springboard for metacognition after the information is reviewed and discussed. Once the students have a strong background of factual knowledge, during independent time, the teacher can provide tasks, analyze, synthesize, and evaluate the material. The goal is to avoid filling in of missing information on worksheets, even in collaborative groups, because it limits student response since the aim is a predefined, correct answer (Nystrand et al., 1993). Their findings indicate that offering a variety of peer-led discussion formats aimed at getting students to negotiate answers, convey their impressions of what they have read, or co-create a representation of their reading selections as good for inspiring a variety of ways to approach a text, even when the students in the class ostensibly have low or limited literacy skills.

Various activities that can be used are:

1. *I Have a Question, Who Has the Answer.* The students are divided into two teams in their small groups in which one half of the team develops questions for the other half of the team. The questions that are developed include student justification of their answer.
2. *I Have a Plan.* Students are asked to develop a plan for the German air force to attack Great Britain. Each table team develops a plan. After a plan is developed, it is shared with classmates.
3. *Concept Map for Germany.* Based on the facts the students researched, they show the relationship of the facts to a big concept. In the center of the map is the big concept with supporting ideas surrounding the big concept. This arrangement can be thought of as "hub and spoke" with the hub being the big concept and the spoke being the facts.
4. *Big Concept Map for England.* This is the same activity as big concept map for Germany but from the English point of view.
5. *Analyze This.* Students are given a fact which they have to analyze. For example, develop a plan of Germany attacking England. How would it work? What would they do?
6. *Analyze This.* Germany attacked France and won. What is the next step and why?
7. *Pro and Con Grid.* Students make a "T" chart and write down the pros and cons of the concepts developed from the facts.
8. *Create a Timeline for Facebook Using the Facts.* Create a timeline for Facebook using the facts. Alter some of the facts and create a new timeline.
9. *Re-write History to Create a Netflix Show.* Create a show for Netflix using the assumption that Germany was successful in the Battle of Britain. Use facts and data from Germany's previous victory in the Battle of Britain.

When the students work in small groups, the task is to encourage discussion, testing of hypotheses, and idea testing. There exists evidence that in secondary classrooms where there is a free exchange of ideas regularly takes place during discussions, the results show higher achievement in classrooms in which such exchanges rarely or never take place (Applebee et al., 2003). These findings are consistent across tracking levels, with the free exchange of ideas being highly effective for low-track as well as high-track classrooms (Applebee et al., 2003; Nystrand, 2006, Nystrand, M. (2006). Research on the role of classroom discourse as it affects reading comprehension.

After I Ask Questions, How Will I Respond to Students?

An important aspect of classroom interaction is the manner in which the instructor handles student responses. When asking questions, the critical fact is: what the student is doing as a result of the question asked.

When an instructor asks a question, students can either respond, ask a question, or give no response.

Strategies to Use When Students Respond

Reinforcement: The goal of reinforcement is to confirm, if correct, what the student states; validate the student's response and encourage future participation. The response can be verbal or nonverbal. Keep in mind the nonverbal response can be as important as the verbal response. Even more important is the fact that the nonverbal response can be very telling, such that a verbal positive response with a nonverbal expression can trigger a negative feeling.

The teacher can reinforce correct student responses by making a positive statement and supporting the statement with a positive nonverbal communication. Examples of nonverbal responses include smiling, nodding, and maintaining eye contact.

Improper nonverbal responses included looking at papers while the student speaks, not looking at the student or seeming not interested as she is speaking. If the student response is incorrect, the teacher has to ensure that the correct information is attached to the incorrect response otherwise everyone, including the student, will remember the question and incorrect response.

The task is to "connect" the student response to the correct question. So, if the teacher asks: "Who was involved in the Battle of Britain?" Suppose the student responds: "The German Army and British." The teacher has to correct the response by telling the class that "the Battle of Britain was an Air Battle for England. The battle was an attempt to determine air supremacy so the German forces could compel Britain to agree to a negotiated peace settlement. It was a battle in which the Royal Air Force (RAF) and Fleet Air Arm (FAA) of the Royal Navy defended the United Kingdom (UK) against large-scale attacks by Nazi Germany's air force, the Luftwaffe. It has been described as the first major military campaign fought entirely by air forces. So, the battle was not fought on land. If, I was to ask about the Battle of France on the other hand, it was a battle that involved land and air support."

After reinforcement is provided, the teacher can explain the answer to the rest of the class. For example, "Does everyone share the same view? If not, who has a different perspective?"

Reinforcement is important as it validates the student's answer and provides support for the student. Throughout the lesson, the teacher should keep in mind that metacognition strategies need to be taught. When teaching metacognition, the teacher should keep in mind that there are three general phases for metacognition: planning, monitoring, and evaluating (Tanner, 2012).

Let's look at the three stages of metacognition as it relates to the teacher and the student for developing questions.

Planning Phase: The teacher collects data from the lesson, from the students via a Consolidation for Closure or formative data from active monitoring. (The phases are delineated in Dr. Barbiere's texts *Setting the Stage: Delivering the Plan Using the Learner's Brain Model* or *Activating the Learner's Brain: Using the Learner's Brain Model*, 2018.)

Planning Phase for the Teacher: For the teacher the task is to ask questions which will help the student understand what the short- and long-term goals are for the lesson being taught, help them tie in prior knowledge, and what strategies to use. So, the questions can be: "Does everyone understand what our short- and long-term goals are for today? I have posted the Student Learning Target on the board as that is our short-term goal for today while the Essential Question is our long-term goal."

As I teach the lesson, as yourself: Does this make sense? How will I use the information I am learning? During the lesson also think about your prior knowledge about the subject and how it relates to what we are learning. For example, I know this because it is related to x which we studied. The questions to ask yourself are: How are they related? How are they different? Finally, how will I use my notes to increase my knowledge of the new material? So class, as you take notes, think of how the information will be helpful. Ask yourself: Is this information useful and important?

Planning Phase for the Student: As a student, I will need to know exactly what we are learning today and how it ties to the "big" picture or long-term goal. Do I know and understand exactly what we are learning today that I can take the Student Learning Target and re-state it in my own words? As the teacher teaches the lesson, will I tie it to my frame of reference? If not, will I ask the teacher to clarify any confusion?

Informational Stage

Informational Stage for the Teacher: This phase of the teacher's planning involves how the teacher will use questions during the three phases of instructional delivery—direct instruction, small group, and independent time.

Direct Instruction: During this phase there are two different approaches the teacher can take. One approach is for the teacher to provide information to the students, so they are prepared when they work in small groups by having the facts and knowledge they need to do the task. The other approach, which is used in math classes, is to provide the students with a problem to solve. The students work on the assignment and when they need help, they ask the teacher. The teacher uses the request as a "teachable moment." She can ask the class to see how many other students had the same problem and work with a small group as a "skills group."

Or, if most of the students are having the same problem, the teacher can provide large group instruction; Since the students are asking for help, they have a vested interest in attention to the instruction. The teacher's lesson makes sense and has meaning to the student as she needs information to resolve her problem. The teacher can model the problem for the student and walk her through the process or use "oral rehearsal" and share her thinking throughout the process. "I have this problem, so the first thing I would do is x because y." Then, throughout the process the teacher continues the dialogue providing a rationale to students to help frame their thinking.

Teachers' Role During the Direct Instruction Phase: During this phase, the teacher is providing information to the student, so the questions have to determine if the student knows the information. Her questions probe the students, that is, can you explain in your own words the information that I shared with you? How would you use the information? As I share information with you, think: how can I use this information? The teacher's task is asking questions that probe the students and to help students take the information and apply it.

Using analysis and synthesis type of questions helps students develop metacognition, that is, What evidence can you find? Think about the relationship between x and y as you get the information; think about how this information can be applied.

Students' Role During the Direct Instruction Phase: During this phase, students are getting information. So, during the instructional delivery, the student will be using the information in small group or large group discussions. The information becomes the building block for subsequent learning, so the material has to make sense. Since students will be using the material at a later time, the material has "meaning."

During this phase, students can use "elaborative investigation" The strategy is one that focuses on enhancing memory by activating prior knowledge or by seeking understanding by encouraging students to generate "why" questions after reading material. Once the question has been generated, students try to derive possible answers that define the cause-effect relation between subject and the predicate. In this method, students are engaged in a process of active learning and seeking relationships.

Teachers' Role During Small-Group Instruction: During this phase, students are processing the information that was presented in the direct instruction phase and applying it to solve a problem or complete a task. It is during this phase the teacher moves from "instructor" to "facilitator" by asking questions to promote student thinking. The probing questions can include: "Can you explain …?", "How did you arrive at this conclusion?"

Effective Probing Question

- Allows the student to think about what they are doing and provide multiple possible responses showing that the student has spent time thinking about the problem.
- Promotes discussion by avoiding questions which require a yes or no response, as a quick yes or no terminates robust discussion.
- Stimulates reflective thinking with how, why, are there other ways to approach this task?
- Challenges student assumptions.
- Seeks to develop meaning.
- Promotes further investigation of the problem.
- Challenges student thinking.

During small-group instruction the teacher has to monitor student learning and by asking questions and assessing student progress. A common mistake is to think the students are busy on the task because there is a lot "of discussion." The students may be engaged and noisy but they can be off topic and talk about other things not related to the topic. Hence, the teacher must do "active monitoring," purposeful assessment of progress keeping active records of student's progress which will be used for planning subsequent lessons.

Consolidation for Closure: This is the last chance the teacher has to collect data from the students as it is done at the end of the lesson. Closure is not to be confused with review. The rule of thumb is that if the teacher is doing the talking, it is review, for example, today we talked about x. Or, the teacher will spend the last five minutes of class reviewing what was taught. Closure on the other hand is student talk. The teacher will have the student tell her three things they learned today.

Closure is also an important process for the learner because the learner will summarize what has been learned and engage in the process of attaching sense and meaning to the learned information. The talk and summary by the student will provide information to the teacher who can ask clarifying questions to the student to help them see relationships and develop understanding. When a teacher asks clarifying questions to a student at the end of a lesson, the purpose of the questioning is to help the student re-frame their thinking and/or look at their thinking with a fresh sense of eyes.

When doing Consolidation for Closure, the teacher can use overt or covert closure strategies. Examples are provided in table 4.5.

Whatever the style that is employed, the important task is to ensure that the student is doing the talking.

Responding to Students

Wherever the teacher is in the instructional delivery process, the teacher has options for responding to students. In its most basic structure, there are three basic modes that can be used. They are *reinforcement* (when the response is correct), *probing* (when the student needs help in getting to an answer), and *realigning* (when the answer is incorrect, the teacher has to align the answer to the correct question or realign the student response to the correct stem so the student and the class will hear the question and correct answer). How many times have teachers reported that students will recall what was stated in class which was incorrect because, "I heard it in class"? They made the connection because that is what they heard which makes the case for "realignment."

Reinforcement: As stated above, reinforcement of correct answers is very important. Consequently, when the answer is correct, the teacher should provide positive feedback to the students. The teacher should keep in mind that her feedback, even if it is positive, will be undermined if she sends a nonverbal clue which is negative. Unfortunately, any negative nonverbal clue will outweigh any positive comment. So, a smile, head nod, and eye contact go a long way as will rolling your eyes.

Nonverbal clue of not maintaining eye contact with the student, looking down, or shuffling papers let students know that you really are not interested even though positive praise is used. Likewise, a negative comment with a positive nonverbal cue sends a mixed message to the student but not as bad as a negative comment with negative nonverbal cue.

Some of the more common forms of verbal praise are "good job" or "I like the way you do." Positive feedback, such as a smile or nod of recognition, is used to reinforce students for appropriate behavior. According to Little & Akin-Little, 73 percent of teachers used positive touching (e.g., a pat on the back), and 63 percent sent a positive note home to parents (2008). They report that a further 60 percent used stickers or tokens and 53 percent

Table 4.5 Examples of Overt and Covert Activities

Overt	Covert
Tell Me in Your Own Words: Students are asked to paraphrase what they learned.	Tell a Friend: Students work in pairs and share what they learned.
Tweet: Students send a tweet to the teacher. They have to consolidate what they learned in 3–5 keywords.	I have an answer, who has a question? Students write a question in which the answer captures the critical component of what they learned.
Red Light, Green Light For elementary students, each desk has a red or a green cup. The teacher will ask the class who agrees and if they agree, the student will turn the green cup upside down.	Signals: Students work in teams of three and share what they learned. A spokesperson is selected for the group and they share what was discussed. The rest of the class gives a thumbs up or thumbs down if they agree or disagree.
Brainstorm: Students share their one takeaway from the lesson and come to a consensus on the critical elements of the lesson.	Thesis Statement: Students summarize what they learn and then consolidate the information into a thesis statement.
Whiteboards: Students use the whiteboard to write critical points of the lesson.	Exit Tickets: Students write on an index card what they learned from the lesson. The key take away points.
Think, Pair, Share: Students work in small groups, share their information, and then share it with the larger group.	Writing Conference: Students are given three questions to answer then pair-share with a buddy what they learned. The summarize what they learned and share it with the class. The student selects one key point to write about at home.
Four Corners: Teacher list a key point to the lesson and posts the key point at a corner of the room. Students select which of the four points they like and go to the particular corner of the room that has their point listed. They develop a summary statement from their small-group meeting.	Response Logs: Students write in their response log what they believe are the critical elements of the lesson. The teacher reviews the logs and gives the students feedback.
L & A Chart: Students write what they learned and how it can be applied.	Student Checklist: The teacher has several questions she asks the students and their answers are noted on a checklist.
Key Words: Students wite key words from the lesson.	Short Summary: Students summarize what they learn in three sentences.

provided students demonstrating appropriate behavior with extra privileges (such as additional computer time or recess time) (Little & Akin-Little, 2008). Unfortunately, positive praise, that is, good job, great, excellent, is well received by students as they like to hear good news but is not effective for providing feedback as feedback needs to be specific so the student knows exactly what was done to earn the praise that was given.

Probing: The middle ground between a positive response (providing reinforcement) and correcting an incorrect one (re-alignment) is probing (when the answer is partly correct or superficial). When the student provides a response that the teacher feels could be "scaffolded up", the teacher will ask additional questions until she gets the correct response. By using probing questions, the teacher can help the student to critically analyze her own thought. Probes start where the teacher analyzes the student statement.

For example, when Mr. Thompson asked about the Battle of Britain, the students did not know who was fighting in the battle so he asked factual questions. He could have provided a fact sheet for the class to refer to so they all would have a frame of factual information. Then, when he said "I think I've been placing too much emphasis on details. What I want you to do now is forget about memorizing things. I want you to *think* history, okay?" He could have asked: "What are some ways that Germany could attack England?" The students would reply: by air, land, or sea. His follow-up activity would be to have three groups—an air, land, and sea group to discuss how they would attack and share their finding with the class.

- To help students *develop understanding, assumptions, and ideas*:
  - Teacher can ask the class: "What would you need to know if you were going to attack by air, land, or sea?"
  - Student: "By air, I want to know if they have an air defense. By land, I would need to know where the best landing site is and by sea, I would need to know what navel defense they have."
  - Teacher: "What assumptions can you make and what should you not assume? Think about those questions as you plan your attack and as you plan your defense."
- To help students *deduce relationships*:
  - Teacher: "Compare and contrast what you need to know as you plan your air, land, or sea attack. What is similar or different for each mode of attack?"

To clarify or elaborate on their comments:

Mr. Thompson asked: "What county did Roosevelt want to supply with weapons?"
Student: "Britain."

Table 4.6   Questions to promote an attack by Air, Land or Sea

Air	Land	Sea
How do we defend against an air defense?	How would they defend a land attack?	What do we need to prepare against an attack by sea?
What is the advantage of our plan over a land assault or sea battle?	What is the advantage of our plan over an air attack or sea battle?	What is the advantage of our plan over an air attack or land assault?
What is the disadvantage of our plan?	What is the disadvantage of our plan?	What is the disadvantage of our plan?
Where would the air attack take place and why there?	Where would a land assault take place and why?	Would the sea battle be close to land or further out to sea?
Do we have air superiority? If we don't, what will we do if the air attack penetrates into the country?	How many soldiers would be needed for a land assault? Check other land assaults by Germany to determine a reasonable number of troops.	What would it take to launch a successful attack by sea?

Teacher: "Does everyone agree? Turn and talk with your neighbor for reasons why the United States wants to support Britain."

Note: The question that was asked was a factual question and required a single response. To promote student thinking, the teacher would ask the class: Why would the United States want to support Britain? This question promotes students to thinking about major concepts. The students will be asked to justify their responses.

   Possible probing question stems:

• As you do your research, think about the different ways the problem can be solved. Think outside the box for different and creative ways to solve the problem.
• How is the land strategy different than the sea or the air strategy?
• Ask "why" this will work? For example, "Why will this work?"

Realign: (When the answer is incorrect, the teacher has to align the answer to the correct question.) This is an important process in responding to students because in the reinforce and probing stage, the student has the correct answer or partially correct answer. In this phase, the students do not have the correct answer so they need guidance to get to the correct answer. First, the answer and question have to be joined so all the students may have the correct information.

After the "attachment" is made, the teacher has to take the student to the correct stage. Teacher: "Now that we have that question answered, let's focus on our original question which was X."

Now that we have three different ways to respond to students, let's talk about possible strategies that the teacher should or should not use.

Should I or Should I Not?

We talked about the responses students give and how the teacher reacts to the response. Now let's look at strategies that the teacher should or should not do after the student responds to the question.

1. Don't provide the answer to your own question. Too often in an effort to move discussion, the teacher will answer her own question. This is usually the case if it is getting close to the end of the class period and the teacher wants the students to know the information. Alternative: If is it getting close to the end of the period, the teacher can pose a question to the students to answer for home learning and write their answer on an index card. The index card will be an "admit" ticket to class the next day.
2. Don't ask a series of questions in an effort to get students to know factual information. It may be easier to have a fact sheet for the students to refer to during the class. The author had an experience while doing a learning walk to observe a teacher for a twenty-minute period and she asked forty-five questions. Her response to me was that she wanted the students to have facts. I asked if she felt that they retained the facts. She replied yes and volunteered to ask the class the next day the facts. Regrettably, the students only remembered a few facts and tuned out as the questioning continued.
3. Answer the question for the student but make them think it was their idea. Teacher: "Who fought in the Battle of Britain?" Student: "Not sure." Teacher: "Do you remember if it was Germany and England?" Rather than provide the answer, the teacher can ask the student to "phone a friend" to get help or a clue.
4. Do encourage students to ask, "what does this mean?" when they are reading textual information.
5. Encourage students to see connections and relationships to what they know and what they are learning. How does this fit in to what I am studying? Or, is this important to know and why?
6. Encourage students to self-regulate their learning. Teacher: "If you don't know the answer, use the resources in the room, ask a friend, or use the internet before you come to me to ask for help."

7. Use "wait-time" when responding to a student so it gives them time to think. There is research that has been done on "wait-time" (See Rosenthal and Jacobson research on wait-time.)
8. Be mindful of equity when calling on students, boys and girls, general education, or special education students, etc.
9. Do refer back to the Student Learning target or Essential Question throughout the lesson to help the student make sense of the lesson.

In order to help students self-regulate their learning, encourage them to ask reflective questions. Examples include:

1. Why is this fact or information important?
2. How can you explain in your own words what you are reading?
3. What do you know already that you can apply to the new knowledge?
4. Think about an argument you can make against what you are reading. I agree with this because? I disagree with this because?
5. What evidence will I use to support my claim?
6. What will I do if I need help?
7. How will I monitor my progress?

After the assignment is completed, students can ask themselves:

1. What are some possible implications of this?
2. How can I summarize the information in three sentences?
3. How can I apply this information?
4. What data will I use to defend my answer?
5. I know this material because I can?
6. The information made sense to me because?
7. The information is useful to me because?

Teacher prompts after the assignments are completed:

1. How did you arrive at that answer?
2. What claims will you use to support your answer?
3. How would you use this concept in real life?
4. What problems did you encounter?
5. What will you do differently if you had to do the assignment again?

SUMMARY

When developing your lessons, remember that there are four stages of the process: the planning process, reediness stage, informational stage, and closure. Each phase has a different purpose so the teacher has to be mindful of the kinds of questions that can be used (and planned). The key is planning. Specifically, each phase will require specific questions to make the phase productive for the student. In the next chapter we will be looking at activities to do with the students or for administrators to use with their staff.

REFERENCES

Applebee, A. N., Langer, J. A., Nystrand, M., & Gamoran, A. (2003). Discussion-based approaches to developing understanding: Classroom instruction and student performance in middle and high school English. *American Educational Research Journal, 40*(3), 685–730.

Blosser, P. E. (1991). *How to ask the right questions.* Washington, DC: National Science Teachers Association.

Briggs, Saga. (2014). Socratic questioning: 30 thought-provoking questions to ask your students. *Blog*, November 8, 2014, taken from: Informed. Retrieved from www.opencolleges.edu.au/informed.

Flavell, J. H. (1979). Metacognition and cognitive monitoring: A new area of psychological inquiry. *American Psychologist, 34*, 906–911.

Heron-Hruby, A., Trent, B., Haas, S., & Allen, Z. C. (2018). The potential for using small-group literature discussions in intervention-focused high school English. *Reading & Writing Quarterly, 34*(5), 379–395. DOI: 10.1080/10573569.2018.1457459

Little, J. G., & Akin-Little, A. (2018). Psychology's contributions to classroom management. *Psychology in the Schools, 45*, 1–9. DOI: 10.1002/pits.20293

Math Forum. *Fermi questions: A Louisiana lesson web activity in collaboration with the math forum.* Retrieved from mathforum.org/workshops/sum96/interdisc/sheila1.html. 1996.

Nystrand, M. (2006). Research on the role of classroom discourse as it affects reading comprehension. *Research in the Teaching of English, 40*(4), 392–412

Pintrich, P. (2002). The role of metacognitive knowledge in learning, teaching, and assessing. *Theory Into Practice, 41*, 219–226

Questioning Strategies. (2016). Questioning strategies. Center for Innovation in Teaching & Learning. University of Illinois. Jan. 07, 2016. Retrieved from https://citl.illinois.edu/about-citl

Rosenthal, R., & Jacobson, L. (1968). Pygmalion in the classroom. *Urban Review, 3*, 16–20. DOI: 10.1007/BF02322211

Rosenthal's Work on Expectancy Effects. (n.d.). *University of Wisconsin - Madison Psychology Department.* Retrieved April 18, 2013, from http://psych.wisc.edu/braun/281/Intelligence/LabellingEffects.html

Schraw, G. (1998). Promoting general metacognition awareness. *Instructional Science, 26*, 113–125.

Schweigert, W. (1991). Classroom talk: Knowledge development, and writing. *Research in the Teaching of English, 25*(4), 469–496, 470.

Spiegel, A. (2012, September 17). Teachers' expectations can influence how students perform: Shots - health news: NPR. *NPR: National Public Radio: News & Analysis, World, US, Music & Arts: NPR.* Retrieved April 22, 2013, from http://www.npr .org/blogs/health/2012/09/18/161159263/teachers-expectations-can-influence-how -students-perform

Tanner, K. (2012). Promoting student metacognition, Vol 11, 113–120 September, 2012. The American Society for Cell Biology. Retrieved from http://creativecom-mons.org/licenses/byy-nc-sa/3.0

Thompson-Grove, G. (n.d.). Pocket guide to probing questions. School Reform Initiative. Retrieved at: http://schoolreforminitiative.org/doc/probing_questions _guide.pdf.

Wong, H., & Wong, R. (2004). *First days of school.* Mountain View, CA: Harry K. Wong Publications.

Wragg, E. C., & Brown, G. (2001). *Questioning in the primary school.* London and New York: Routledge Falmer.

Chapter 5

Questioning Activities

TEXTBOX 5.1

What is the focus of this chapter?

This chapter will focus on strategies and activities to determine effective questions and how activities can be used to determine question effectiveness.

Focus Questions:

1. How will I incorporate self-regulation principles or strategies into each phase of the instructional process?
2. How can I link my questions to developing a growth mind-set?
3. How can I evaluate my questions for each stage of instructional delivery using the Learner's Brain Model for lesson planning and delivery?
4. When planning questions, how will I incorporate self-regulation principles and growth mind-set strategies into each phase of the process?

INTRODUCTION

When teachers plan their lessons, there are activities and strategies they can use to plan the kinds of questions to use and to assess their effectiveness. The frame of reference will be to develop student self-regulation and to promote a growth mind-set mentality. The outline of this chapter will be to use the four stages of the Learner's Brain Model, developed by Dr. Barbiere as a template for the lesson plan. Details about the Learner's Brain Model can be found in two books by Dr. Barbiere: *Setting the Stage: Delivering the Plan Using the Learner's Brain Model* and *Activating the Learner's Brain: Using the Learner's Brain Model.*

Let's briefly look at the overall game plan for questioning as it relates to student self-regulation and questioning to promote a growth mind-set. Since there is a lot of research on self-regulation and growth mind-set, we will look at a specific research which is tied to questioning to promote both.

How Do we Promote Self-regulation During the Planning Stage?

The Planning Stage is the most important stage as the teacher uses information from both formative and summative assessments to plan the lesson. During this phase, the teacher will be planning the lesson from start to finish. More importantly, the teacher will plan what questions to use during each phase of the planning.

The Planning Stage uses from the formative assessments during the lesson and from closure. During the phase, the teacher has to ask herself:

1. What is the data telling me?
2. What do I notice?
3. Are there any trends?
4. Were there some areas where more students performed better? Performed worse?
5. Will I need to provide small-group instruction based on the information that I have?
6. Should I plan for direct instruction for the large group?
7. How will I remind the students to self-regulate their learning?

Some possible self-regulation strategies for the teacher during the Planning Stage are:

1. Remind the students to check their work.
2. Remind students to use resources to help them solve their assignments.
3. Remind students to think about what they have to accomplish so they do not spend time on collaterial or unnecessary information.
4. Remind students to use their friends or resources in the classroom if they have a problem.
5. Remind students to check their work. "I will check my work and use rubrics to determine if I am on track."

6. Remind students to organize their material, make notes, outline so they can refer back to it at a later date.
7. Encourage students to make connections.
8. Remind students to link what they know with the new learning.
9. Remind students to keep their material organized.

Growth mind-set task for the teacher to use for the Planning Stage. The teacher will be providing students with strategies to promote a growth mind-set. These strategies are:

1. Remind students that the brain is malleable.
2. Remind students of the power of "yet."
3. Remind students not to give up if they are having problems and to seek out other solutions.
4. As students do their work, have them think of the possible ways to expand their knowledge.
5. Remind students to keep a journal so they can refer back to it.
6. Remind students that if they are experiencing a challenge while doing the work, they should look up to the challenge as an opportunity to try something new and different or to look at different ways to approach solving the problem.
7. Remind students to reflect as they do their assignments.

Growth Mind-set tasks for the student to use:

1. Remember: If I am having difficulty during the lesson, I will not give up and remind myself that I may not have the answer yet but I will figure it out eventually.
2. I will set a goal and work toward that goal.
3. I will use all the resources at my disposal to be successful
4. I will use rubrics to assess my progress and to provide input to me for I would need to do to achieve the goal.
5. In order for me to get to a deeper understanding of the concepts, I will analyze the data for the purpose of using the information to make assumptions and projections for how the data can be applied. Once the analysis is done in the classroom, we often see students moving to higher levels of thinking on their own—creative types move to synthesis and critical thinkers gravitate toward evaluation. One way to expand the thinking is to make a "claim" and think about what evidence is needed to support the claim.

Activity

My claim _____
Evidence
1.
2.
3.
Counterclaims?_____

The Goal of Growth Mind-set During the Readiness Stage. During this stage the teacher is introducing the new material and trying to tie it to the student's prior knowledge. The brain needs to make the connection. Think of the piece of information as an "orphan" or a stand-alone bit of knowledge. If the "orphan" information is tied to familiar information, it no longer is an "orphan" but has a friend that she can "hang with." A connection is made. So, as a teacher, the task is to help the student's brain make connections.

How does the teacher promote growth mind-set during the Readiness Stage?

1. The teacher will remind the students that they are learning new information and try to see the relationship of what they learning to what they know. Encourage the students to ask themselves: How is this connected to what I already know?
   How is this related to what I already know?
2. Remind students that if the new information is hard to comprehend, there are strategies they can use to retrieve information to help them solve the problem.
3. Remind students that they have the power of the class and to use their classmates if they are having problems.
4. Remind students that if they are having problems, "failure" can be seen as an opportunity. Your thinking with respect to 'failure' is that if you don't know something, you have an opportunity to get more information to learn about it. Think of it as an opportunity for growth.
5. As you face challenges, celebrate your successes. Be happy with your small victories as small victories lead to big victories.
6. Remember, if you have a problem and seek help from a friend, be prepared to accept the feedback that is given. Look upon the information you receive as "feedback" and not as "criticism." If you view it as criticism, you are less likely to "hear" or accept the feedback you are given.
7. Remember to keep track of your progress and what works and what needs to be refined.

How does the teacher promote self-regulation during the Readiness Stage?

1. During the Readiness Stage, remind students that they have the power to regulate and monitor their learning. As they are working on the assignment, remind the students to "self-regulate" their learning.
2. Remind the students to use the resources in the room if they are having problems.
3. Remind students that they can use their friends or classmates as resources to help them work our problems.
4. Remind students to keep a journal so they can refer back to it after the assignment is competed so they can know what works and what needs to be changed.
5. Reminds students to take breaks as exercise helps with metacognition.
6. Remind students of self-regulation skills: "Remember if you are having problems to use the resources and your classmates as a reference source. Please do that before you come to talk to me."
7. In order to reduce stress with new information, remind students to "cognitive reframe." Basically, reframing is a way of changing the way one looks at something and, thus, changing your experience of it. Remind student to cognitive reframing a stressful event into a challenge or opportunity to self-manage and regulate their learning to get the desired results. "Reframing" will help the student to refocus their learning to becoming empowered.

How does the student promote growth mind-set during the Readiness Stage?
During this stage, the material is being presented and the student will not only have to make sense of the material but know what to do if and when she experiences difficulties. Hence, the student needs to understand what a growth mind-set is and the power of "yet." In order to help the student understand the "growth mind-set" the teacher is to model growth mind-set practices and give the students the strategies they need to use.
    Examples are:

1. Encourage students to use growth mind-set vocabulary—I can, I didn't get it yet but I will, etc.
2. If I get stuck, I will . . . .
3. I will try alternate strategies if what I am doing does not work.
4. What will I do differently if I have a problem?
5. Remember: Mistakes help me learn.
6. I will accept the challenge.
7. I will never stop trying.
8. I will be focused and try my best.

9. I will use a growth mindset so mistakes will help me learn.
10. I got this!
11. There are many paths I can take but it may take time to find the correct path.

How does the student promote self-regulation during the Readiness Stage? During this stage, new material is being introduced so the student will need to interpret the information and start to plan what to do with the information. Planning ideas can include:

1. As a student I will gather any information needed to complete the task, including the new information I am learning.
2. After I have all the information, I will set a goal of what I want to accomplish.
3. After I set my goals, I will monitor my progress and use any resources in the room as a reference. I will remember to believe in myself and realize that I can find what I need.
4. I will remember to focus on the task at hand and if I start to drift, I will go for a walk or do some physical activity to help me focus.
5. I will remember to self-monitor my learning by using a scoring guide or rubrics to monitor my progress.
6. As I monitor my progress, I will remember to reinforce those strategies that have been working by journaling my experiences and creating a log of "successes." This will help me know what is working and what needs to be refined as well as giving me confidence knowing I can achieve my goals.
7. At the end of my class period, I will reflect on what worked and what needs to be corrected.

The goal of growth mind-set during the Informational Stage. During this stage, the teacher will be employing a "gradual release" model of "I do" (teacher gives direct instruction to provide background information), "We do" (models the lesson and provides a practice for the students), and finally "You do" (the students do independent work). The Informational Stage (Dr. Barbiere's Learner's Brain Model described in *Setting the Stage: Delivering the Plan Using the Learner's Brain Model* or *Activating the Learner's Brain: Using the Learner's Brain Model,* 2018) will focus on instructional delivery in large- and small-group settings.

How does the teacher promote growth mind-set during the Informational Stage?

Direct Instruction: During this phase it is important that the teacher models a growth mind-set so students will know what to do during their independent time. She can:

1. Explain to students that the information is new so don't give up if there are problems or challenges along the way.
2. Don't forget to challenge yourself.
3. Growth Mind-set Chart

What Can I Do?

The following are small-group activity and cooperative learning strategy suggestions for a teacher to promote a growth mind-set. When assigning small groups or using cooperative learning activities, remind students to use the power of the group to help resolve problems:

1. Organize groups based on ability level and remind students that there are many talents in the group so to use the power of the group to get to "yet" when they are stuck.
2. Organize groups by various skill levels and tell the group that students in the group have various skills to check with each other if there are problems as one of your colleagues may be able to help you. First, try to resolve your problems on your own before you seek help from your colleagues.

Table 5.1   Instead of a Fixed mindset use a Growth Mindset of What can I do?

Instead of—	What can I do?
Waiting for the teacher to get help when I am stuck, I —	Ask a friend or use the resources in the room.
Stopping when I have a challenge or difficult task, I—	Set short-term goals to accomplish parts of the assignment.
Sitting at my desk doing nothing because I don't know a specific rule or operation to use, I—	Use resources or ask a friend.
Thinking how am I doing, I—	Use rubrics to assess my progress.
Giving up, I—	Take a break and come back to the assignment with "fresh eyes" and mind-set.
Quitting, I—	Take a break to see where I am having problems so I can plan a new approach.
Saying I'm done, I—	Check my work to see what I can do to improve my work.
She is smart and she is done with the assignment	I'm smart and I go at my own speed to solve problems
This is too hard, I—	This is a challenge but I will figure it out.

3. Keep the groups small so the teacher can monitor the group to assess student progress and so individuals in the group can participate. Ask the students: "What are you learning today?" "How did you challenge yourself?" "Are you satisfied with your work or are you going to try to improve it?" "Is everyone trying hard?" and "What will you do if you have problems?"

4. Remember that cooperative learning should be constructed for a purpose not to have an activity where students are doing a project or activity in groups. It is ineffective when it is not purposeful, planned, and guided. An activity which is not planned is an activity; an activity which is planned is a purposeful activity because it will lead to something.

5. Small cooperative groups are more effective when the activity is planned and all students have the opportunity to participate. Ensure that each group member has a specific role and there are protocols for everyone to have a "voice" and an expected outcome.

6. Use "active monitoring" with the group as there is a tendency for one person to control the group. With active monitoring, the teacher asks questions to ensure that the students are on task and not just "off track." During this phase it is not a "check in of how are you doing" but an assessment of how they are doing.

7. With a strong personality in the group, students may defer to a strong personality or not even contribute so the teacher should assign everyone a role and make sure that each person has to report.

Questions for a teacher during student independent time. During this time, the teacher has the opportunity to question students to assess their progress and to promote a growth mind-set for students who are struggling. Possible questions are:

1. Mistakes are an opportunity to grow. What growth opportunities have you had today? Did you learn anything from the experience that will help you in similar circumstances?

2. When you were stuck, how did you get unstuck? Did you use different strategies?

3. Did you ever think that you would give up when you were having problems? If you did, what did you do to get back on track?

4. What did you change as you progressed and what did you keep? How did you determine what to keep?

5. Do you feel you are making progress? I am proud of you for sticking with the task even though you had some problems.

6. Did this activity enhance your brain function? How?

7. During the activity did you encourage your classmates?

8. What did you learn from the activity?
9. Did you think it would take long to complete? What will you do differently next time, or what have you learned that you will use next time?
10. Did you ask for help or were you able to get a resolution to your problem?

How does the teacher promote self-regulation during the Informational Stage? During this phase, teachers will strive to make the students develop skills and strategies which will help them self-regulate their learning. The goal is to make them self-dependent and not teacher dependent. Teachers need to teach with metacognition.

> Teaching with metacognition refers to teachers' thinking about their own thinking regarding their teaching before, during, and after conducting lessons to increase instructional effectiveness. Teaching for metacognition indicates that "teachers think about how their instruction will activate and develop their students' metacognition, or think about their own thinking as learners. (Hartman, 2001, 149)

1. Remind students that they must use all available resources or *ask a friend for help*, before asking the teacher a question. (Remind students: TBM or Two Before Me.) This is a necessary step for self-regulation so students know that going to the teacher when they have a problem is not a good strategy as it forces the students to rely on going to the teacher before even trying to solve a problem. The process encourages students to look inward and to themselves to solve problems.
2. Remind students to make careful observations of their ecosystems. After the observations, they will record their answers in their journals. They will use the rubrics to self-manage and self-monitor their answers.
3. Remind students to keep records that describe their observations or observations which were done by other students that were successful. Remind students to carefully distinguish actual observations from ideas and speculations and write key concepts.
4. Encourage students to talk to their peers who were successful to see what strategies they used and how they decided upon those strategies. "Why did you do and why?"
5. Instruct the students to manage their time wisely. Remind them to monitor their time and keep focused as they have control over their time management.
6. Remind students that note keeping is a form of self-management and a very important self-regulation strategy because students can refer to their notes at any time or use the note to study. More importantly, there are various programs that can be taught for note taking, that is, Cornell Notes

so students need to know the different methods that are available. Note taking skills are important or else students will be writing every word the teacher is saying and not pay attention to the lesson.

7. Encourage students to use technology in the classroom (the district may provide laptops or computer carts with student computers for student use) or their laptops. The goal for the students is to use technology to self-manage their learning by seeking out resources on the internet.

8. Encourage students to actively search for information during their independent time and once they get the information, interpret it and then monitor their progress.

9. If the students are going to conduct a science investigation, remind them that precise record keeping is crucial to the replication of the process of the experiment.

10. During any investigation process or information-seeking process, remind students to reflect upon their actions and methods, by continually asking "why" and to be prepared to justify their activities and answers when the teacher is doing her active monitoring. The "why" helps the student dig deeper into the process to gain understanding.

11. Encourage students to collaborate and communicate ideas with their peers, as well as to extract information from posters, rubrics, exemplars, or instructional charts in their surrounding environment. Remind students that they can and should "environmentally" self-monitor (using the classroom environment) their learning.

12. Discuss collaboration and communication as forms of self-regulation.

13. Remind students they have the power to achieve.

14. Remind students that "metacognition," "cognitive monitoring," and self-regulation are all tied together.

15. When working in small groups or having discussions, have folks "expand" their answers.

How does the student promote growth mind-set during the Informational Stage? During this phase, students will be working on their assignments. Since the material is new, students may have a difficult time processing the material and, consequently, encounter problems. They may feel frustrated during this process and want to give up but they must use a "growth mind-set" and not give up. As a student, they should:

1. Do I have all the information?
2. What am I missing if I don't understand what I am doing?
3. Do I think this is my best product or can I do better?
4. Do I have a Plan B in case things go sideways?

5. I will remember that I can improve.
6. I will not give up but will think about different strategies if I get stuck because mistakes will help me grow.
7. I will change my words and this will help me change my mind-set. Deeds not words.
8. I will find a way to solve the problem or make a way to solve the problem.
9. I may start slowly but I will finish.
10. Don't think that that the task is impossible but that it is possible.
11. I will strive to improve.
12. I will take risks.
13. I will use multiple strategies to solve the problem.

How does the student promote self-regulation during the Informational Stage? Once the student knows that she will be using a "growth mind-set" during the process, the next step is to have the student self-regulate her learning. Having a growth mind-set encourages the student to try and not accept defeat while self-regulation encourages the student to feel empowered and seek out help using herself as a resource and not relying on someone else or the teacher. Possible strategies include:

1. I can do this so I will use whatever resources I need to use to be successful. I will use the power within me to resolve any challenges or problems I have.
2. I will set goals for myself and work toward the goals, monitoring my progress along the way. I will use all available resources to monitor my progress.
3. The teacher told me that student's use of self-regulation learning strategies promotes academic achievement so I will remember to regulate my learning as it will promote my achievement.
4. I will monitor my performance throughout the lesson.
5. I will list specific behaviors so I will be able to monitor my progress.
6. Remember, I will try my best and will not give up when I am faced with challenges.
7. When I face challenges, I will change my language from negative comments to a positive statement, that is, change "this task is too hard" to "I will use face the challenge and come up with a plan."

The goal of growth mind-set during the Closure Stage. During the Closure Stage, the teacher and the student have the last chance to process information, consolidate the information, and provide important data which is correct so when the student goes to the next class or home, the teacher wants the student to leave with correct information. This is very important as the brain consolidates information when one sleeps so it is important that correct information is consolidated.

How does the teacher promote growth mind-set during the Closure Stage? It is important that the teacher lets the students talk so she can assess what the takeaway from the lesson was from the student's point of view. It is critical that the teacher ensures that students have the correct information when consolidation for Closure is done because "providing participants with misleading information after the encoding of an event can revise the original memory (misinformation effect)" (Loftus, 2005).

There are many types of activities which can be used for overt or covert strategies; in addition, visual, auditory, kinesthetic, or tactile strategies can be used. There are a variety of closure activities that teachers can do but more importantly, it requires "student talk." If it is teacher talk, it is "review." Below is a form which can be used as an "exit ticket."

The teacher will use various forms of closure to provide students the opportunity to share information. She can use covert or overt methods of

Table 5.2   Exit Ticket Sample. Student adds her notes

Exit Ticket: What I Learned?	What Do I Need to Know?	What Will I Do If I Get Stuck?
Notes		

Table 5.3   Samples of Overt and Covert Exit tickets

Overt	*Covert*
Tell Me in your Own Words: Students are asked to paraphrase what they learned.	Tell a Friend: Students work in pairs and share what they learned.
Tweet: Students send a tweet to the teacher. They have to consolidate what they learned into 3–5 keywords.	I have an answer, who has a question? Students write a question in which the anser captures the critical componet of what they learned.
Red Light, Green Light: For elementary students, each desk has a red or a green cup. The teacher will ask the class who agrees and those students who agree will turn the cup upside down.	Signals: Students work in teams of three and share what they learned. A spokesperson is selected for the group and they share what was discussed. The rest of the class gives a thumbs up or thumbs down if they agree or disagree.

closure and based on the student's responses, provide strategies or suggestions to promote a growth mind-set.

Samples of overt and covert closure activities are presented in table 5.3.

(A complete list of overt and covert examples of closure, as well as, visual, auditory tactile, and kinesthetic similar to those below can be found in Dr. Barbiere's book: *A Field Guide for Activating the Learner: Using the Learner's Brain Model*, Rowman & Littlefield, 2018.)

How does the teacher promote self-regulation during the Closure Stage? During this stage, the teacher is gathering information and encouraging students to use their own resources to try to solve any problems they may encounter. Since the teacher will not be readily available to students, it is important for the teacher to remind students to use all available resources. The teacher can say:

1. You will be working on your own so if you have problems, use resources that I have provided to you, the internet, or your peers.
2. If you have tried to find the answer to your concerns, make a note of the problem and we will discuss your problem and how to solve it.
3. If you are stuck, take a brain break and walk away for five minutes to clear your thoughts.
4. We will use an "Entrance Ticket" for tomorrow's class as you will write something you learned from the assignment and how it can be used. If you had a problem, write down the problem and what you did. The class will try to solve your problem.
5. Remember, you are a superhero and the power is within you!
6. Use your colleagues so if you are having problems, text a friend.
7. If several students are having a similar problem, form a study group.
8. Reframe the problem to look at it through a different lens.
9. If you are stuck, ask yourself: "What can I do differently?"

How does the student promote growth mind-set during the Closure Stage? During this phase, the student has processed information from the lesson and reports to the teacher how the information was processed. During the phase of instruction, it is important that the student provides information to the teacher as the teacher will use it to assess student knowledge and to plan the next lesson. During this phase it is important for the teacher to process the student information to determine how much the student knows and to encourage the student if they seem to have limited knowledge of the subject.

So, during this phase the student's growth mind-set is more the result of the teacher's questioning and prompting to encourage the student to try when they do their independent work.

Table 5.4   Characteristics of Visual, Auditory, Kinesthetic and Tactile learners

Visual	Auditory	Kinesthetic	Tactile
Characteristics: Use visual materials, that is, maps, pictures; write; illustrate; read; use color graphs; and flowcharts	**Characteristics:** Lectures, discussions, debates, create mnemonics characteristics	**Characteristics:** Attend labs, take frequent breaks, move, assemble collections	**Characteristics:** Use printed sources; take detailed notes; use manuals, handouts, or story starters
Use of *whiteboards* *Graphic organizers* *Mind maps* *Drawing* *Picture* *The purpose is to have students express what they learned using a variety of modalities.*	Inventive Dialogue: **Three "Whats"** *Students respond to the following:* <u>*What did you learn*</u> *today?* <u>*What does it mean*</u>*? (How is this important? relevant? useful?)* <u>*What can you do with the information*</u>*? (What is the practical application of the information?*	Turn and Talk: **Come to My Side** *Students are arranged in two lines facing one another. Students discuss main points of the lesson to try to convince members from the other line to come to their line.* **Four Corners** The teacher has a critical point noted on paper and posted in the four corners of the room. Students select a critical point and stand in the corner which has the point which they support.	Student Checklist: **Quick Write Likert Scale** *Students respond to teacher-generated prompts (perhaps displayed on the overhead projector or on a permanent poster in the room. The prompts are from a difficult level to an application level* 1. *I can apply today's lesson in the real work* 2. *Today's lesson makes sense to me because* 3. *I understand today's lesson because* 4. *I enjoyed today's lesson but I have some questions* 5. *I found today's lesson difficult because*

How does the student promote self-regulation during the Closure Stage? During this phase, the student will tell the teacher that this is what I learned today and when I do my independent work, I will use all available resources to overcome any challenges I may have.

SUMMARY

This chapter addressed the following questions:

1. How will I incorporate self-regulation principles or strategies into each phase of the instructional process?
2. How can I link my questions to developing a growth mind-set?
3. How can I evaluate my questions for each stage of instructional delivery using the Learner's Brain Model for lesson planning and delivery?

In this chapter, suggestions for teacher growth mind-set and self-regulation for each phase were provided. Additionally, suggestions for a growth mind-set and self-regulation strategies for teachers to use during each phase of the instructional cycle were provided.

The next chapter will address developing questions for various types of tests.

REFERENCES

Anderson, L. W., & Krathwohl, D. R. (Eds.) (2001). *A taxonomy for learning, teaching, and assessing: A revision of Bloom's taxonomy of educational objectives* (Complete ed.). New York: Longman.

Barbiere, M. (2018). *Activating the learner's brain: Using the learner's brain model.* Lanham, MD: Rowman & Littlefield.

Barbiere, M. (2018). *A field guide for activating the learner: Using the learner's brain model.* Lanham, MD: Rowman & Littlefield.

Bloom, B. S., Engelhart, M. D., Furst, E. J., Hill, W. H., & Krathwohl, D. R. (1956). *Taxonomy of educational objectives: The classification of educational goals. Handbook I: Cognitive domain.* White Plains, NY: Longman.

Brookhart, S. (2010). *How to assess higher-order thinking skills in your classroom.* Alexandria, VA: ASCD.

Clark, D. A. (2014). Cognitive restructuring. In S. G. Hofmann & D. Dozois (eds.) *The Wiley handbook for cognitive behavioral therapy, first edition.* New York: John Wiley & Sons, Ltd. DOI:10.1002/9781118528563.wbcbt02

Flavell, J. H. (1979). Metacognition and cognitive monitoring: A new area of cognitive-developmental inquiry. *American Psychologist, 34*, 906–911. DOI: 10.1037//0003-066X.34.10.906

Hartman, H. J. (2001). Teaching metacognitively. In H. J. Hartman (ed.) *Metacognition in Learning and Instruction* (pp. 149–172). Boston, MA: Kluwer Academic Publishers.

Hupbach, A., Gomez, R., Hardt, O., & Nadel, L. (2007). Reconsolidation of episodic memories: A subtle reminder triggers integration of new information. *Learning and Memory, 14*: 47–50.

Locke, E. A., Shaw, K. N., Saari, L. M., & Latham, G. P. (1981). Goal setting and task performance: 1969–1980. *Psychological Bulletin, 90*, 125–152.

Loftus, E. F. (2005). Planting misinformation in the human mind: A 30 year investigation of memory. *Learning & Memory, 12*: 361–366.

Marzano, R. J., & Kendall, J. S. (2007). *The new taxonomy of educational objectives* (2nd ed.). Thousand Oaks, CA: Sage.

Marzano, R. J., Pickering, D., & McTighe, J. (1993). *Assessing student outcomes: Performance assessment using the dimensions of learning model.* Alexandria, VA: ASCD.

Morin, A. (2020). Using cognitive reframing for mental health. Retrieved from https://www.verywellmind.com/reframing-defined-2610419

Pressley, M., Borkowski, J. G., & Schneider, W. (1987). Cognitive strategies: Good strategy users coordinate metacognition and knowledge. *Annals of Child Development, 4*, 89–129.

Xu, W., Carifo, J., & Dagostino, L. (2012). Constructing a metacognitive knowledge framework for post-secondary EFL reading teachers' summarizing strategies instruction with expository text: A case study, phase. *Creative Education, 3*(Special Issue), 829—839. Published Online October 2012 in SciRes (http://www.SciRP.org/journal/ce).

Zimmerman, B. (1990). Self-regulated learning and academic achievement: An overview, *Educational Psychologist, 25*(1), 3–17. DOI: 10.1207/ s15326985ep2501_2

Zimmerman, B., Bandura, A., & Martine-Pons, M. (1992). Self-motivation for academic attainment: The role of self-efficacy beliefs and personal goal setting. *American Educational Research Journal, 29*(3). Retrieved from https://doi.org/10.3102%2F00028312029003663

Zimmerman, B. J. (1989). A social cognitive view of self-regulated academic learning. *Journal of Educational Psychology, 81*(3): 329–339.

Zimmerman, B. J., & Martinez-Pons, M. (1988). Construct validation of a strategy model of student self-regulated learning. *Journal of Educational Psychology, 80*, 284–290.

Chapter 6

Planning Questions

TEXTBOX 6.1

What is the focus of this chapter?

This chapter will focus on strategies and activities to determine effective questions. When do I use (1) multiple choice, (2) true/false, (3) matching, (4) short answer, (5) essay, and how will activities be used to determine question effectiveness?

BACKGROUND

As teachers develop assessments, what kind of questions should be used and, more importantly, what types of assessments are most desirable for achieving a specific goal? For example, if the teacher wants to determine if a student understands facts, then a multiple-choice type of test would be an effective way for the student to show her knowledge of facts. Let's look at the technical aspects to consider when determining the qualities of a test.

Technical Quality of a Test

When developing a test, there are technical qualities that need to be considered. So, let's look at the technical considerations when developing questions. Some of the technical considerations to consider are cognitive complexity, application of content, value of the information, standards-based language, application and transfer of the material, reliability of the test.

Cognitive Complexity

When developing tests, the teacher wants to determine the level of cognitive complexity that will be sought from the test. If the teacher uses Revised Bloom's Taxonomy (RBT) as a guide, the level of complexity can be assessed depending on Bloom's level of questioning. So, if information is being sought, then knowledge types of questions that recall information, knowledge, or facts. So, the types of questions will ask students to define, explain, label, name, match, recall, list, state, or match. These types of questions will elicit memory of material that was taught by recalling facts, terms basic concepts thereby providing the teacher with information on what the student knows.

As a teacher, developing a multiple-choice quiz can be useful so, suggestions, tips, dos, and don'ts will be shared later after we talk about the other technical qualities of testing.

Application of Content. Depending on what the teacher is looking for from the students, the teacher may want to determine if it is lower levels of metacognition of factual recall or higher levels of cognition which is the application of concepts. The concern for these kinds of questions is that the students must have the information to be able to tie the facts together, understand concepts and apply the concepts in a meaningful, practical manner. The concept of application is not new as teachers feel more comfortable when they know that kids can apply what they are learning so the material that is taught has meaning. Absent any application or meaning, kids are inclined to ask: "Why are we learning this?" or "Is this going to be on the test?" What they are really saying is if the material has no meaning, why are they learning this?

Using an application assessment will enable the students to see how what they are learning can be applied so learning facts and figures has application. In some cases, for math instruction, the teacher may start with a problem and let the students work on the problem to try to solve it. At some point, they will need direct instruction, so they are more inclined to ask for help or be receptive to the teacher providing instruction since they need the information to complete the problem.

Another technical concept is *Value of information.* This concept is closely tied to the application of content as seeing the value of information is in the application of the material. The value is directly tied to the application. In order for information to go to long-term storage, it requires presenting the material, so it makes sense to the student and more importantly, presenting the material so it has meaning. Sense and meaning are two critical factors for long-term retention.

When presenting material, the teacher ties in value and application, so students see the importance of the material.

Standards-Based Assessments. There is a relationship between standards-based instructional planning and standards-based assessments. Teachers use a standards-based curriculum in their instructional to promote high expectations. When wring for the State of New Jersey turning around low-performing schools, one of the biggest problems that I encountered was the use of a "watered down" curriculum. The fear was that a standards-based curriculum would be too hard for the students, so teachers used a curriculum that was not as challenging. Unfortunately, when the time came for the students to take the State Assessment which was standards-based, the students did poorly. Teachers were upset that the students seemed to do well on their assessments, but the assessments were not tied to standards. When the teachers reviewed the testing data and did an item analysis, much of what they taught was not on the test. It was a true wake-up call for teachers to spend teaching skills and only to have these skills not being tested. It was a valuable lesson for teachers to realize that a standards-based curriculum is expected and desired when developing the curriculum.

Teachers did realize that they can bundle standards and teach using an interdisciplinary approach, so the skills are tied together in a meaningful manner.

Application and Transfer. For this kind of assessment, students are asked to transfer what they know or apply facts and information. This type of assessment involves students solving problems. Students can make models and a presentation to write a script for an interview. For this type of assessment, teachers may consider having students do a portfolio assessment.

Reliability. Whatever the form of assessment that is planned, it is important that the test is reliable. The test must represent what the student actually knows and not the result of students guessing answers. There are considerations to ensure test reliability which will be discussed for the various kinds of tests that are planned.

Let's look at the various kinds of assessments that can be used, the advantages and disadvantages of each, and tips in test construction.

What type of test should I use? The answer to this question is what do I want to assess? Once I answer that question, I can plan what type of assessment I will use.

Multiple-choice Assessment. The multiple-choice question assessment has advantages and disadvantages. There are tips to avoid when constructing such a test. So, let's look at the advantages, disadvantages, and tip construction to determine if this assessment is a type of assessment that should be used and when it is most effective.

- When to use: Multiple-choice questions are best used for checking whether students have learned facts and routine procedures that have one, clearly correct answer. The student will have to know the correct answer as each question has only one correct answer.

Multiple-choice tests have often been accompanied by increased emphasis on basic skills, whereas performance-based assessment has been associated with greater focus on problem solving inquiry (Cimbricz, 2002; Smith, 1991; Vogler, 2006; Looney, 2009). Ehren et al. (2019) found that elementary school teachers in Boston and New York targeted their instruction on differences in item format within the same test. Teachers looked at how students performed on multiple-choice and open-ended responses. Teachers looked at student responses to the response sections and provided various instructional strategies to target those format types.

Doing an item analysis of the questions that are asked will be a powerful tool for teachers to determine what students know. Additionally, teachers can ask students to develop test questions as part of a readiness for the test. The teacher can ask students to bring in test questions as an entrance ticket to class. For example, the teacher can say "Class for tomorrow's entrance ticket brings a question you think should be on the test on a 3 × 5 index card with the answer on the back." The teacher will collect the index cards at the door when students enter and shuffle the cards. As a review, the teacher will pull a card and ask the class the question. Depending on how many students answered the question the teacher will be able to assess the class.

Or, the teacher can ask the class, how many other students had a similar question like this for the test?

To encourage student input, the teacher can select a few questions that were not read in class and put them on the test. The students will love seeing that the question that they wrote was actually placed on the test and hopefully the writer of the question should get that question answered correctively (See the scatter gram in table 6.1).

Table 6.1 Scattergram of responses to 10 teacher questions

Question	A	B	C	D	E
1					X
2				x	
3	x				
4		x			
5			x		
6		x			
7			x		
8					X
9				x	
10	x				

Advantage

Preparing a multiple choice does have advantages. The test is relativity easy to develop, easy to score, and can include a broad range of topics to test the depth of student knowledge. Depending on the test construction, the range of questions that are proposed can provide valuable information on the depth of the student's knowledge, assuming there were no test construction problems.

Disadvantage

The positive of being able to construct a relatively easy test is also a disadvantage. The ability to develop a quick, easy test may lead the teacher to make mistakes in the test construction. For example, the ease of developing a test may lead the teacher to construct sentences that can only have one answer because it is the only answer which is grammatically correct.

Another disadvantage of multiple-choice questions is the teacher had a pattern of correct responses. For example, if all correct answers are "B," the student will be more inclined to use answer B if she is not sure of the answer. To avoid this problem, the teacher must review all the answers to make sure that there is a balance of answers and not an overabundance of one correct answer. A simple chart will show the spread of answers (and it can be used as an answer key).

Tips

When developing multiple-choice assessments be mindful of the following:

1. The grammatical structure of the sentence can only be one answer that is possible.
2. There is not an overabundance of one number for an answer, that is, nine out of ten answers are "B." This will immunize guessing.
3. If one is looking for factual recall, then a multiple-choice test would be an effective assessment. It can also be used as a pre-assessment to see what the students know—a baseline data point.
4. Have multiple answers to avoid students just picking or guessing, which is the correct answer.
5. After the assessment, review answers to ensure that students have the correct information.
6. Use a variety of scoring strategies, that is, points taken away for incorrect answers. Students get points for correct answers and points deducted for incorrect answers so rather than guessing, they leave the answer blank and get fewer points deducted. The student can see how confident they felt when answering a question. After they see the results of the test, they

can determine their level of confidence for each answer. Answers that were incorrect can be and area that the student can examine to determine what the lack of confidence was or if there were two answers that were closely matched that the student could not make the correct choice and had to guess. The student can also look to see what the mode was of studying for the assessment to determine if the model was successful and made the student feel confident. If the student did poorly and had a low confidence level, then he or she should look at other ways of preparing for the assessment, so she has more confidence.

Confidence levels: 90+ = high; 70–90 = moderate; 50–70 = low.

Regarding confidence levels, students can review their answers to determine if they changed their answers from correct to incorrect or from incorrect to correct. Researchers investigating answer changes on objective test items have consistently shown the preponderance of changes to be from wrong to right (Schwarz et al., 1991; Crocker & Benson, 1980; Payne, 1984). Something told the test taker to review her answer to make sure it is the correct response before completing the assessment. What was it?

So, why is it that most students change their answers? The researchers report that they change answers either because of rereading or rethinking an item. In addition, answer change seems to be particularly effective in answering moderately difficult or difficult items correctly (Stough, 1992). However, low test scorers do tend to use this strategy ineffectively (Schwartz et al., 1991), changing answers more frequently and less successfully.

7. Use the results of the assessment to do an item analysis (see Table 6.2). The item analysis will tell the teacher to see how many students had an

Table 6.2 Data to use form 10 questions to do an Item analysis

Question	A	B	C	D	E	Confidence +1 0. -1
1					x	
2				x		
3	x					
4		x				
5			x			
6		x				
7			x			
8					x	
9				x		
10	x					

item correct and how many had an incorrect answer, in which case they may need to be re-taught or explained more completely.

8. Avoid using terms like always or never.
9. Be mindful of the length of the answers as students may think the longer answer is the correct answer.

True/false: If multiple-choice questions are easy to grade and easy for the student, then using a true/false type of assessment is even faster as there are usually only two answers for the student to select as opposed to four or more answers which are used in a multiple-choice assessment. So, let's look at the advantages, disadvantages, and tips for true/false tests.

In a traditional true/false question, students are asked to judge whether the statement is true or false. True/false questions are best suited to assessing surface-level knowledge but can be crafted to assess higher-order thinking. Like multiple choice, students can process and respond to true/false quickly, allowing the test designer to assess more content areas in an exam. The test can also be longer as it does not take long for the student to respond to the question.

Although true/false questions are easy to determine, traditional multiple choice is thought to be superior to true/false for several reasons, including:

- Students have a higher probability of guessing the right answer in true/false responses as there is a 50-50 (1 out of 2) chance of guessing the correct answer compared to a multiple-choice question where the probability is 25 percent (1 out of 4).
- True/false questions offer little insight into why students may answer incorrectly as it may be a lack of knowledge or a lucky guess. This disadvantage is an advantage if the teacher just wants to see the depth of factual knowledge a student has.
- True/false questions are necessarily absolute; it can be difficult to write questions that are unambiguously true or false. A tip that students look for when answering a true/false question that it must be all true to be true.

When to use: True/false questions are best used when a teacher wants to know the student's judgment/comprehension about a fact, concept, example, principle, or other content-based items. The information is important as teachers need to know if the student knows the information. Factual information base and information are needed by the student as it will enable him or her to analyze, synthesize, or evaluate future data. Matters of opinion or interpretation are not good subjects for true/false items as the teacher is determining student knowledge base.

Advantages

True/false question. Compared with multiple-choice questions, research suggests that the Multiple True/False formats provide a more complex picture of student thinking regarding the various options while requiring virtually no additional question writing or scoring efforts (Couch et al., 2018). However, we do not want to rule out multiple-choice questions as there are two cases in which the multiple-choice format would still be appropriate. The first situation occurs when the answer options are mutually exclusive, such that answering one option negates the other options. This is useful as the student has to know the correct answer so she can rule out the incorrect answer.

The second situation occurs when the instructor wants students to make comparisons among response options. For example, instructors in clinical medicine might ask students to select the best treatment plan among several viable options (Chandratilake et al., 2011). Nonetheless, when the answer options contain different—even if closely related—conceptions, the Multiple True/False formats provides the most direct way to assess student understanding of these ideas.

In developing Multiple True/False questions, the teacher develops a question stem followed by a series of prompts or statements that students evaluate as being true or false. In one way there is a similarity of the Multiple True/False question to Multiple-Choice questions in which students "select all that apply." The big difference is that the teacher can have the student mark each statement as correct (true) or incorrect (false). Using this option, the student has to know the material and be able to know how each answer is true or false.

Hubbard et al. (2017) found that the rate of correct responses to Multiple True/False questions correlated with the rates at which students listed the corresponding conceptions in Free Response answers.

Disadvantages

When researcher (Couch et al, 2018) compared the Multiple True/False with the Multiple - Choice format, the percentage correct in the MTF format. On average, students answered the Multiple-Choice format correctly 67 percent of the time, whereas a similar group of students provided a fully correct answer in the Multiple True/False formats only 36 percent of the time. Thus, although many of the students were given full credit in the Multiple-Choice format, only about half of these students would have been able to demonstrate complete question mastery when asked to evaluate all the response options.

There are several disadvantages of Multiple True/False questions:

1. There is a high percentage in favor of the student guessing the correct answer; especially if the student has the only option of true or false, the odds are 50-50 that she can guess the correct answer.

2. Since there is a high probability of guessing the correct answer, the teacher really does not know if the students know the material or if they were able to guess correctly.
3. There are three types of true/false questions—(i) classic statement with true/false options, (ii) changing a false statement to make it true, and (iii) cause and effect (Chavez & Millard, 2012). Depending on the type of question being asked, the teacher can build in safeguards to ensure question validity.
4. True/false questions can be used for assessing low-level questions.

Tips

There are several tips that can be used when developing true/false questions. These include:

1. Students are taught to approach each statement as if it were true and then determine if any part of the statement is false. Just one false part in a statement will make the entire statement false. So, when constructing sentences, vary true and false statements so students don't always start with the premise that the question is true.
2. Students know that if just one part of the sentence is false, then the entire sentence is false. A sentence may be mostly true because it contains correct information, but it is ultimately false if it contains any incorrect information. Teachers can build into false statements to mix with the true statement. Or teachers may ask students to make a false statement true or say why a statement is false. This information will show the teacher what the student knows.
3. Be mindful of qualifiers or keywords that provide clues to the correct answer. Qualifiers are words like sometimes, few, often, frequently, never, generally, or seldom. The use of qualifiers will tip off the student so they should be avoided. Sometimes, few, and often usually reflect true statements, while always and never reflect a negative statement.
4. Be mindful when constructing the assessment with the use of negatives. Students are taught to drop the negative word and then read what remains. Without the negative, determine whether the sentence is true or false. If the sentence (without the negative) is true, then the correct answer would be "false."
5. Be mindful of using long sentences because long sentences often contain groups of words and phrases separated or organized by punctuation. Students are told to read each word set and phrase individually and carefully. If one word set or phrase in the statement is false (even if the rest are true) then the entire statement is false, and the answer is "false."

6. Guard against educated guesses by either deducting points for incorrect answers so students will not be inclined to guess and will leave the answer blank if they don't know.
7. Be mindful of the length of the question stem as there is a greater likelihood that the statement will be false with a long stem because it only takes one part of a statement being false to make the entire statement false. The longer the statement, the more chance one part will be false.
8. When constructing stem questions, consider using Revised Blooms Taxonomy when developing the questions. Depending on the student activity, specific questions can be developed. For example, for a knowledge question, the task is for the student to remember information, for example, "Who wrote *Huckleberry Finn*?" (recall of a fact). If the teacher is looking for application, the question will ask the student if the concept was used correctly, for example, a list of scores, that is, 77, 81, 79, 91, 93, 94, and 73 is provided and the answer asked if the mean of the numbers is 84. The students would have to know how to find the mean from a list of numbers. For evaluation, information is provided and the student must establish if the criteria are correct or incorrect.

Matching. Matching assessment allows the use of a smaller sample size, as there are two columns for the student to match one column with the second column. Matching questions consist of two columns, typically one column on the left and one on the right. The column on the left is known as "Clues" and the one on the right is known as "Matches." The objective is to pair the clues on the left side with their matches on the right.

When to Use: According to Benson & Crocker (1979) in *Educational and Psychological Measurement*, students with low reading ability scored better and more consistently with matching questions than the other types of objective questions. They were found to be more reliable and valid. Consequently, a matching assessment does not have to be long. The teacher will prepare the students beforehand for keywords and phrases and then provide an assessment using the words with the correct answer.

Advantage

There is one big advantage of using this kind of assessment:

1. The teacher can cover a lot of material based on the amount of time spent to construct the questions ratio. Since the tests are short, they can be used as "formative assessments" for the teacher to assess student knowledge and understanding.
2. The short assessment will allow for great flexibility as various samples can be used.

3. The teacher can use the assessment as a baseline of the learners' knowledge.
4. This type of assessment works best with assessing low levels of cognition.
5. Since the student has to match the clue with the "match," there is less of a chance of guessing the correct answer compared to other question types.
6. Great for users who have a lower reading level as there are few words to read so comprehension is not a determinant in assessing student knowledge.
7. Less chance for guessing than other question types as there is a correct answer for each "clue."
8. Since the test is short, many assessments can be used and the tests can cover a large amount of content.
9. Since students are reading long massages for compression and because the clues are short and an answer is available, it is easy to read for the test taker.
10. The length of the test makes it easy to grade.
11. Studying for this kind of a test requires association—knowing facts because the match is provided in the answer column.

Disadvantage

1. This test is really designed to determine the student's factual knowledge. Unlike other tests, teachers cannot use these tests for students to apply the knowledge they have learned or analyze information.
2. These tests can only be used to assess "low-level" knowledge or knowledge about a specific subject as there are specific clues and matches for each clue.
3. These tests are better used at the elementary level as they assess student information. At the elementary level, matching questions works quite well as the information being tested is basic. However, as a course increases in complexity, it is often difficult to create effective matching questions

Tips

Hints for Creating Effective Matching Questions

1. Although it may seem easily understood, the teacher has to ensure that there are clear directions in how the teacher expects the student to complete the assessments. The directions for a matching question need to be specific as there are 10 clues and 10 matches. The directions need

to clearly state whether an item will be used once or more than once so students know how to plan to use the "matches."

2. Matching questions are made up of "clues" (left column) and "matches" (right column). The teacher can use the exact number of matches equal to the number of clues or, the teacher can have more matches than clues, so the student has to know the correct answer. Another possibility is to have more matches, but the clues may have more than one match. More responses should be included than premises. For example, if you have ten clues, you might want to include ten, twelve, or fourteen matches.

3. The match column and the clue column should be short and organized in a logical manner. The teacher can list everything alphabetically, numerically, or chronologically.

4. Avoid unnecessary words or phrases and keep the list short.

5. Be mindful that the test is designed to be short, so the teacher gets a quick read based on the information.

The next type of test construction that teachers can consider is short answer type of questions. We will discuss when to use this kind of assessment, advantages, disadvantages, and tips in test construction.

Short Answer. The short answer assessment has an advantage over multiple choice as the multiple-choice format provides the student with a prompt to "jar" his interest. Multiple-choice tests have often been accompanied by increased emphasis on basic skills, for example, recall of facts or bits of information addressing Revised Bloom's Taxonomy of "remember" which is to recall facts and basic concepts. However, performance-based assessments have been associated with greater focus on problem solving and inquiry (Cimbricz, 2002; Smith, 1991; Vogler, 2006; Looney, 2009).

The short answer is the next type of assessment. It allows for a wider and more complex range of student answering to allow for students to share their thinking.

When to Use: When the teacher wants the student to show her thinking by answering a question as opposed to providing the student with an answer and having the student select the correct answer, the short answer format is the better option. A short answer format requires the student to create an answer. Short answer is commonly used to assess the basic knowledge and understanding (low cognitive levels) of a topic. The data from the assessment will give the teachers an indication of how much the student knows and what informational data needs to be provided. Short answer exams determine students' ability to remember information and apply knowledge.

Advantages

1. Short Answer Questions are great for teachers who do not want to spend a lot of time grading tests because they are easy and fast to grade. They are not as fast as true/false assessment which is one of the fastest assessments to grade.
2. Short Answer Questions can be easily constructed as they do not have to have many questions.
3. Short Answer Questions can be used as test prep for essay question assessments as the structure of short answer questions is very similar to the essay question format. Teachers can have students practice taking short answer assessments so they feel less anxious when they take the essay assessment.
4. Unlike true/false assessments, there is no guessing of the answers, students must supply an answer. With the true/false assessment, the student has a 50-50 chance of guessing a correct answer and with a four-part multiple-choice question, there is a 25 percent chance of guessing the correct answer.

Disadvantages

1. The biggest limitation of the Short Answer Questions (SAQ) is that they can be answered with short responses. Unless there is a rubric or specific answer for the questions, students will feel that what they answered is correct and they should receive partial, if not, full credit.
2. Short Answer Questions are typically used for assessing lower levels of knowledge, as students are required to provide a short response. Hence, a student's study strategy may involve her memorizing questions and answers, so the study processes the same as used for rote memory.
3. Short Answer Questions are not geared to assess deeper learning, that is, analysis, synthesis, evaluation, or creation. Having said that, this disadvantage can be an advantage if the teacher wants to develop skills for taking essay assessments.
4. Students who have poor handwriting or weak spelling skills will find this type of assessment difficult so the results of the test may not be a true measure of their ability.
5. For students with processing problems or spelling/handwriting problems, there can be time management issues when answering Short Answer Questions.

Tips

1. For the teacher, she should prepare the student to understand concepts to build factual knowledge into conceptual knowledge as students will need

to understand facts to expand them into conceptual. Keep in mind Essential Understandings as they focus on the Big Picture. For the student, it means to study for understanding, that is, to understand concepts and Big Picture as you will be asked to provide a short, concise answer. So, even if you can't remember a specific term, if you have a general understanding of the concept in question, you can still be able to develop an answer that is likely to get you full or partial credit.

2. When the teacher is using direct instruction, do not write everything the teacher is saying but the big concepts of the lesson as you need to know what the concepts are to write an answer to the short question. If the student concentrates on facts, there is a possibility of missing the big concepts.

3. Students can use their notes to study by self-testing and doing oral rehearsal, and looking at the notes and thinking what are some questions that may be on the assessment. This process will help the student assess what she believes is important. Additionally, using oral rehearsal will enable the student to hear what she is saying to hear if it makes sense. The process can also help the student think about her answer and think about ways to make it concise. In some cases, the teacher can use a strategy that has the student develop questions to share with the class. "Student Developed Questions" is an effective tool for the teacher as the teacher will see what students believe is important. The teacher can also incorporate the student questions into the assessment.

4. Encourage students to vary their studying strategies. Use notes to make flashcards to have a factual base of information. After the factual concepts are developed, have students develop possible questions so they apply the facts into concepts. Once they know the concepts, they can do an oral rehearsal to answer questions so they can hear how the answer sounds and if anything needs to be tweaked from their answer.

5. If the teacher does not deduct points for guessing, make an educated guess if you are not sure. If the assessment is for math, show your work as teachers want to see your work to determine your thought process in solving the problem. If the assessment is not in math, look at the nouns in the sentence as the nouns usually identify "knowledge" or content. That may help the student understand the concepts being questioned.

6. As with any other types of tests, students are told to answer all the easy questions first so they can spend time with the more difficult questions. If a student spends a lot of time with the difficult questions, they may run out of time and not get to answer the easy questions. Additionally, as you answer the easy questions it may give you information that can be used to answer the difficult questions. Additionally, after you answer the easy questions, determine how much time you have left to answer the difficult ones.

7. As silly as it sounds, read all the instructions first. A colleague of mine requested that students read all the instructions first. The very last item on the list of questions was "answer question one and two only." The students quickly learned to read all the instruction first.

8. As the suggestion was made to read all instructions, the same holds true for reading the question thoroughly as there may be multiple answers that are required. This is especially important if the student believes that the answer is easy and is quick to answer the question without realizing that multiple answers are required.

The last type of assessment that we will be discussing is the essay.

Essay. The purpose of essay type question is to allow students time to organize their thinking and present their ideas. Teachers can assess how students present their ideas (whether the manner of presentation is coherent, logical, or systematic) and how they supported their initial premise. In other words, the student answer provides the structure, dynamics and functioning of pupil's metacognition.

When to Use: When the teacher wants to understand a student's higher-level thinking, essay questions are the best option. The student will answer essay questions by collecting information, organizing the information into a logical framework, and making compelling arguments regarding a position they are promoting and using data to substantiate their answer.

Advantages

1. The format of the essay questions may be few in number, but they are effective for assessing higher-level thinking as the student has to analyze, evaluate, synthesize information, and then make a compelling argument. Their reasoning and logic will become evident in their answer.

2. It is the only means that can assess an examinee's ability to organize and present his ideas in a logical and coherent fashion.

3. It can be successfully employed for practically all the school subjects.

4. Some of the objectives such as the ability to organize ideas effectively, criticize or justify a statement, and interpret, can be best measured by this type of test.

5. Logical thinking and critical reasoning, systematic presentation, etc., can be best developed by this type of test.

Disadvantages

Such tests encourage selective reading and emphasize cramming.

1. Moreover, scoring may be affected by spelling, good handwriting, colored ink, neatness, grammar, length of the answer, etc.

2. The long-answer type questions are less valid and less reliable, and, as such, they have little predictive value.
3. It requires an excessive time on the part of students to write; while assessing, reading essays is very time-consuming and laborious.
4. It can be assessed only by a teacher or competent professionals.
5. Mood of the examiner affects the scoring of answer scripts.
6. There is a halo effect–biased judgment by previous impressions.
7. The scores may be affected by his personal bias or partiality for a particular point of view, his way of understanding the question, his weightage to different aspects of the answer, favoritism, and nepotism.

Tips

1. Knowing your Student Learning Objective and your Essential Question, the teacher has an idea of what was taught and so the essay questions should focus on how kids interpreted the material. In this fashion, you will be working "backward" from what the long-term goal was, how it was reached via the Student Learning Targets to have the student develop an argument based on facts.
2. Ask students to interpret, analyze, and draw conclusions for facts that are presented so as promote student metacognition.
3. Incorporate real-world application in the essay questions so students see the relationship of what they are learning to the real world. The learning will become more meaningful as there will be applications tied to the learning.
4. Use essay questions to see how students reason. This can be done by providing an answer and asking students to explain how the answer was achieved. Knowing what to do is as important as doing it. By explaining their answers, they will know the process and will be able to apply it to a variety of problems as opposed to being able to just do one problem. For example, to understand the process of multiplication they should be able to multiple one digit by one digit or two digits by two digits. Just doing multiplication of one digit by one digit, the students may know that they can continue the process they learned multiplying by one digit to multiplying by two digits.
5. Do not make the questions so broad that it will not assess what the student knows. The goal is for the question to assess knowledge about a specific topic, to create a question that focuses on a specific area.
6. Limit subject matter (create boundaries) so students can organize their thoughts and make a sound argument based on logical reasoning.
7. Use verbs carefully and selectively as the verb drives the action being sought. Therefore, ask students to describe, explain, and justify their answer to elaborate their thinking. For students to interpret data, graphs, or charts,

ask students to analyze or evaluate the data to draw conclusions. Remember, your verbs will provide the reader with direction, so be clear in your request, that is, define, outline, classify, justify, and explain as opposed to broad, open-ended comments like "tell me, what do you think it is?".

8. If there are several questions being asked, place a value on the questions, that is, some questions will be worth more than others as the answer will be more complex so students can budget their time appropriately.

9. If you are constructing two different tests, that is, an A test and a B test, be mindful that it is difficult to construct equal questions so think about what concepts you want to measure and use similar verbs for students to answer the question.

10. Do not start essay questions with words such as who, what, or whether. If we begin the questions with such words, they are likely to be short-answer questions or more appropriate for multiple-choice types and not essay questions.

11. It should be a power test (going for depth of knowledge) rather than a speed test (how many multiple-choice questions can be answered). Allow a liberal time limit so that the essay test does not become a test of speed in writing.

SUMMARY

Specifically, tests of deeper learning are likely to promote desirable changes in practice as the teacher is asking students to demonstrate knowledge and/or application of facts. Knowing the instruction that was provided, the teacher can construct the test to determine the instruction. If the teacher was providing background information as readiness for conceptual understanding, then a multiple-choice test would be an effective vehicle to determine if the students knew the facts. If, however, the teacher wanted to assess comprehension of the facts then an essay type of test would be more effective.

The format of the test sends a message to students. Are students expected to know facts, interpret facts, or use the information as part of a performance? The test is to be an assessment of learning—do students know what was taught and can they demonstrate knowledge?

The test will answer two questions: "Do students know the material?" and "How do I, as the teacher, know she knows it?"

REFERENCES

Assessment Resource Center@HKU (2014). Types of assessment methods. Retrieved from https://ar.cetl.hku.hk/am_saq.htm

Bennett, R. (2011). Formative assessment: A critical review. *Assessment in Education: Principles, Policy & Practice, 18*(1), 5–25.

Benson, J., & Crocker, R. (1979). The effects of item format and reading ability on objective test performance: A question of validity. *Educational and Psychological Measurement, 39*, 381–387.

Berwik, C. (2019). What does research say about teaching. *Eudopia*. Retrieved from https://www.edutopia.org/article/what-does-research-say-about-testing

Black, P., & William, D. (1998a). Assessment and classroom learning. *Assessment in Education: Principles, Policy, & Practice, 5*(1), 7–74.

Brassil, C. E., & Couch, B. A. (2019). Multiple-true-false questions reveal more thoroughly the complexity of student thinking than multiple-choice questions: A Bayesian item response model comparison. *IJ STEM Ed, 6*, 16. DOI: 10.1186/ S40594-019-0169-

Champlin, C. (2006). *A life in writing: The story of an American journalist.* Syracuse: Syracuse University.

Champin, C. (2006). *Strengths and dangers of essay questions for exams.* Pittsburg, PA: Center for Teaching Excellence, Duquesne University.

Chandratilake, M., Davis, M., & Ponnamperuma, G. (2011). Assessment of medical knowledge: The pros and cons of using true/false multiple–choice questions. *National Medical Journal of India, 24*, 225–228.

Cimbricz, S. (2002). State mandated testing and teachers' beliefs and practice. *Education Policy Analysis Archives, 10*(2): 1–21.

Clay, B., & Root, E. (n.d.). Is this a trick question? a short guide to writing effective test questions. Retrieved from https://www.k-state.edu/ksde/alp/resources/Handout -Module6.pdf

Couch, B., Hubbard, J., & Brassil, C. (2018). Multiple–true–false questions reveal the limits of the multiple–choice format for detecting students with incomplete understandings. *BioScience*, 68(6), 455–463. DOI: 10.1093/BIOSCI/BIY037

Crocker, L. M., & Benson, J. (1980). Does answer changing affect test quality? test; types, *Measurement and Evaluation in Guidance, 13*, 233–239.

Disha, M. (n.d.). Essay advantages and limitations/statistics. Retrieved from https:// www.yourarticlelibrary.com/statistics-2/essay-test-types-advantages-and-limita-tions-statistics/92656

Education corner, education that matters, true./false test taking strategies. Retrieved from https://www.educationcorner.com/true-false-tests.html

Ehren, M., Wollaston, N., Goodwin, J., Star J., & UCL Institute of Education. (September 2019). The Nature, Prevalence and Effectiveness of Strategies Used to Prepare Pupils for Key Stage 2 Maths Tests, Final report. (grant number EDO 41601).

Essay test: Types, advantages and limitations/statistics. Retrieved from https://www .yourarticlelibrary.com/statistics-2/essay-test-types-advantages-and-limitations -statistics/92656

Exam questions: Types, characteristics, and ort guide to writing effective test question suggestions. Centre for Teaching Excellence, University of Waterloo.

Exam scoring services. Center for Innovative Teaching and Learning. Retrieved from https://citl.illinois.edu/citl-101/measurement-evaluation/exam-scoring/improving -your-test-questions#essay

Farooqui, F., Saeed, N., Aaraj, S., Sami, M. A., & Amir, M. (2018). A comparison between written assessment methods: Multiple-choice and short answer questions in end-of-clerkship examinations for final year medical students. *Cureus, 10*(12), e3773. https://doi.org/10.7759/cureus.3773

Faxon-Mills, S., Hamilton, L., Rudnick, M., & Skecher, B. (2013). New assessments, better instruction? designing assessment systems to promote instructional improve-ment. Sponsored by William and Flora Hewlett Foundation, published by RAND Corporation.

Hubbard, J. K., Potts, M. A., & Couch, B. A. (2017). How question types reveal student thinking: An experimental comparison of multiple-true-false and free-response formats. *CBE Life Sciences Education, 16*(2), ar26. https://doi. org/10.1187/cbe.16-12-0339.

Kelly, M. (2020). Tips to create effective matching questions for assessments. *ThoughtCo*, Aug. 27, 2020. Retrieved from thoughtco.com/effective-matching-qu estions-for-assessments-8443.

Looney, I. (2009). *Assessment and innovation in education.* OECD Education Working Paper No. 24, EDU/WKP (2009) 3.

McKeachie, W. (2002). *McKeachie's teaching tips* (11th. ed.) New York: Houghton Mifflin.

Millard, S., & Chavez, B. (2012). Writing multiple choice and true/false exam ques-tions. University of Hawaii at Hilo. Retrieved from http://uhhcopfacultyresource .weebly.com/uploads/2/1/9/8/2198211/multiple_choice_and_true_false_exam _question_design_booklet.pdf

Palmer, E. J., & Devitt, P. G. (2007). Assessment of higher order cognitive skills in undergraduate education: Modified essay or multiple-choice questions? Research paper. *BMC Med Educ, 7*, 49. DOI: 10.1186/1472-6920-7-49

Payne, B. D. (1984). The relationship of test anxiety and answer-changing behavior: An analysis by race and sex. *Measurement and Evaluation in Guidance, 16*, 205–210.

Perie, M., Marion, S., & Gong, B. (2009). Moving toward a comprehensive assess-ment system: A framework for considering interim assessments. *Educational Measurement: Issues and Practice, 28*(3), 5–13.

Schwartz, S. P., Mc Morris, R. F., & DeMers, L. P. (1991). Reasons for chang-ing answers: An evaluation using personal interviews. *Journal of Educational Measurement, 28*, 163–171.

Smith, M. (1991). Put to the test: The effects of external testing on teachers. *Educational Researcher, 20*(5), 8–11.

Stecher, B. (2010). *Performance assessment in an era of standards-based educa-tional accountability.* Stanford, CA: Stanford University, Stanford Center for Opportunity Policy in Education.

Stough, L. M. (February, 1992). The effects of test-taking strategy instruction on the processing of test items. Paper presented at the Annual Meeting of the Southwest Educational Research Association, Houston, TX.

Stough, L. (1993). Research on multiple-choice questions: Implications for strategy instruction. Paper presented at the Annual conference of the Council for Exceptional Children (71st,. San Antonio, TX April 5 – 9 ,Information Analysis (070) ERIC copy 302729

Treser, M. (2015). Matching test items: Getting them right. *eLearning Design and Development*. Retrieved from https://elearningindustry.com/matching-test-items -getting-right

Vogler, K. (2006). The impact of a high school graduation examination on Mississippi social studies teachers' instructional practices. In S. G. Grant (ed.) *Measuring history: Cases of state-level testing across the United States* (pp. 273–302). Greenwich, CT: Information Age Publishing.

Writing true-false items. Office of Measurement Services, University of Minnesota Retrieved from http://www.ucs.umn.edu/oms/truefalse.htmlx

Writing true-false questions and evaluating responses. Alabama Professional Development Modules. Retrieved from http://web.utk.edu/~mccay/apdm/mod3at -f_b.html

Xu, X., Kauer, S., & Tupy, S. (2016). Multiple-choice questions: Tips for optimizing assessment in-seat and online. *Scholarship of Teaching and Learning in Psychology, 2*(2), 147–158.

Chapter 7

Putting It All Together

Below is a sample lesson plan and questions that can be used as well as types of assessments to use for planning the lesson. Components of the lesson design use the Learner's Brain Model developed by Dr. Barbiere.

UDL SECOND-GRADE LESSON PLAN FOR UNIT

Title of Lesson Plan: Rainforest Layers and Fruits and Vegetables

New Jersey Common Core Standard:

CCSS.MATH.CONTENT.2.MD.A.2—Measure the length of an object twice, using length units of different lengths for the two measurements; describe how the two measurements relate to the size of the unit chosen.
CCSS.MATH.CONTENT.2.MD.A.4—Measure to determine how much longer one object is than another, expressing the length difference in terms of a standard length unit.

Comments: Having standards provides for the establishment of high standards and will allow the teacher to develop rubrics for students to use. The teacher will remind the class that this is a second-grade lesson plan and as second graders they are expected to put on their "thinking caps" and use second-grade vocabulary and complete sentences when they write.

Standards-based lessons are necessary as the practice of aligning learning to standards helps to ensure that an established higher level of learning is attained based on agreed-upon rigorous standards. Standards promote equity

101

as all students are judged by a measurable standard and not standards relative to various states, classrooms, grades, or schools.

The use of standards also helps guide the teacher in the use of assessments (reference textbook *Setting the Stage: Delivering the Plan Using the Learner's Brain Model* by Dr. Mario C. Barbiere).

To promote metacognition, the teacher will ask questions throughout the lesson to help the students see relationships.

Essential Question

• What is a tropical rainforest?
• What are the characteristics of a tropical rainforest habitat?
• What do all animals need to survive?
• How are plants and animals in the rainforest connected?

"Brain Fact: The essential question is consistent with the brain's processing of visual information in a holistic manner. It is this statement which helps one to see the big picture. In essence, the brain is looking for a pattern in which the visual—'visual thinking'—is connected to the end goal. Basically, the brain is looking to determine if there is a pattern in which a relationship to what is being taught is evident. We know this fact when we are all shown an optical illusion—we look to see a pattern, but the illusion causes the visual impression to be compromised. It is the cognitive process of the new stimuli (the lesson) in the student's current frame of reference that the brain is trying to sort out."

Student Learning Target (SLT) (Objectives): Given a diagram of the rainforest layers, I will be able to identify layers of the rainforest and explain how each layer was formed. I will be able to identify fruits of the rainforest and be able to blend them together to create a balanced recipe.

Comments: As part of the Student Empowerment Program, the teacher will use "I statements" for SLTs so the students develop ownership as part of their understanding of responsibility.

To promote self-regulation, the teacher will have pictures of different fruits and vegetables and sample recipes posted in the room. Some fruits will be from the rainforest so students would need to know the difference.

The teacher will remind the class that there are sample recipes for them to see so they know what to do for developing their recipe. Students are encouraged to use the resources of the room to self-regulate their learning and to empower them.

"Brain Fact: The learning brain needs to link new knowledge with prior knowledge so relationships can be seen and for the information to make sense. Prior to giving the lesson, the teacher should have prior knowledge about the layers of the rainforest. The teacher should also be able to identify various fruits and vegetables that are typically located in the rainforest. The teacher should ensure that the students have a basic understanding of how to effectively measure using a ruler and record the data. Finally, the teacher should have had previous lessons with the students, so they know and are able to explain estimating lengths and making educated guesses."

Demonstration of Student Learning (DSL)

Comments: Student Empowerment—The teacher will remind students that they can use resources throughout the room as they work on their assessment. He will remind students that they can regulate and monitor their learning by using the rubrics and exemplars in the room. He will also remind the class that it is their responsibility.

"Brain Fact: The teacher sets the stage for learning by listing to the SLT and the DSL so the student sees what they will be studying and how they will be assessed. This protocol fits precisely with the current research on the attention mechanisms of the brain. Our brain immediately starts sifting and sorting through all the sensory input. At the same time the brain searches through previously stored information and looks for relevant hooks for the new information. A link to what is being taught and how the learning will be assessed increases the possibility that the brain will search through the right networks and attend to the information that is relevant for a particular topic or issue."

- DSL Logical-Mathematical I will create bar graphs comparing local precipitation levels to precipitation levels in another nation that contains rainforests. I can also make comparisons based upon the graphs that were created.
- DSL Spatial Intelligence I will create a rainforest based on the lecture and my research. An alternative DSL is to create a rainforest poster.
- DSL Linguistic intelligence I will write a newspaper article about the rainforests discussing the pros and cons using research to justify my positions.
- DSL Musical Intelligence I will use the sounds from the rainforest to create a Rainforest CD. The musical interpretation will be scored and shared with the music teacher.
- DSL I will be able to create a recipe using rainforest fruits. I can blend them together for a balanced recipe and justify why they can be blended together.

Comment: The use of various DSL will allow students to activate their "multiple intelligences" or multiple pathways to show they processed the information.

Teacher content knowledge *(necessary prior knowledge)*

Key Vocabulary: Measure, compare, estimate, guess, the forest floor, understory, canopy, emergent layer, mango, guava, papaya, coconut

Comment: Students will research information about the rainforest and develop a list of important vocabulary using "Key List" technique. (Additional strategies are in *A Field Guide for Activating the Learner: Using the Learner's Brain Model* by Dr. Mario C. Barbiere.)

Materials: Rulers, fruits, vegetables, worksheets, iPads, smart board, *The Great Kapok Tree: A Tale of the Amazon Rain Forest* by Lynne Cherry.

Pre-assessment: Students will be asked questions relating to prior knowledge in an attempt to fill out a KWL chart. An informal pretest will be given to help advise instruction and assess students' current levels and knowledge of rainforests.

Comments: The teacher can use questioning prior to taking a test to monitor and adjust instruction based on student's responses. The questioning strategies are done throughout the instructional period to determine if the students know and understand the material, thereby enabling the teacher to pace her lesson.

Additionally, questions can be used for improvement of learning or as a way for students to study. In the former, questions are done during the instructional period by the teacher, and in the latter, questions are provided for home learning as a strategy to help students improve their learning via self-regulation. If the goal is to develop self-regulation-related learners, it is the student who must engage in metacognition to promote self-regulation, self-monitoring, or self-management. (See "Chapter 2: Using Assessments" in *Activating the Learner's Brain: Using the Learner's Brain Model.*)

Readiness Set

Students will be asked a variety of questions regarding fruits and vegetables to activate their prior knowledge.

The questions will involve fruits and vegetables that are typically found in the rainforest as well as locally so students can see the relationship of their local fruit to rainforest fruits and vegetables. Students will also be asked about measuring items and if they have used rulers before to measure anything.

Comment: The Readiness Set has three components: the starter (or a catalyst, hook, attention getter), the connection of what will be taught to what students know, and the tie-in of the new information to the student's prior knowledge. Brain research promotes getting the student's attention and holding it which is one purpose of a Readiness Set. The other purpose of a

Table 7.1   Whole class teaching strategies

Whole-Class Teaching Point

The main concept or big idea is for students to learn and understand that rainforests are valuable and diverse ecosystems. Students will learn that rainforests are composed of various layers and that there are many different types of fruits and vegetables that humans and animals live off of. Examples can be given of some of the different animals in the different layers of the rainforest as well as some of the local tribes that may depend on the rainforest.

NB: Questions at this level are low level seeking to assess the student's knowledge of facts. Recall types of questions. This is important as the goal is to develop factual knowledge. Who, what, why, when, how, recall, state, and identify types of questions would be useful at this level.

Comment: In essence, the brain is looking for a pattern in what the learners see. This pattern seeking is also known as "visual thinking." Basically, the brain needs to determine whether or not there is an evident relationship between to the content being taught and the big picture. The SLT answers the question "What are we learning today?" and the essential question answers the question of why we are learning it. The essential question enables the brain to "see" the completeness. An example of the brain looking for completeness is when we are shown an optical illusion. The eyes search for a pattern but the illusion causes the visual impression to be compromised.

- Highest Level of Understanding: Create
  Students will *analyze and explain* the name of every rainforest layer, as well as provide research on the names and general sizes of all the different fruits and vegetables that may be found in the rainforest. They will be able to present their finding to the class and include creative representations of their findings.

NB: Questioning at this level is to promote thinking, such as questions that encourage students to explain, justify, elaborate, or conclude type.

- Low level of understanding: Recall, understand
  Students will learn all the names of the layers of the rainforest with minimal error (recall) as well as show their understanding of the fruits and vegetables in a rainforest by accurately measuring and comparing at least 75 percent of the fruits and vegetables.

NB: Use recall types of questions at this level. Examples include: cite, label, list, name, state, quote, recall, define, and discuss.

- Essential Level of Understanding:
  All students will learn that rainforests are diverse ecosystems that are composed of layers, with many people and animals that depend on their fruits and vegetables. They will be able to justify why the rainforest is important and explain its value in today's society.

Comment: Another way to understand the Essential Question is to see it as a relationship between the cognitive process of the new stimuli (the lesson) and the student's current frame of reference. This cognitive process is the brain's function, by which it sorts and orders new information. The learner's brain is contemplating and thinking: What is the relationship and what is the pattern? (See *Setting the Stage: Delivering the Plan Using the Learner's Brain Model.*)

Table 7.2   Whole group Lesson Planning

Whole-Group Lesson Planning
1) Creating a Barrier-Free/UDL Learning Environment for Lesson

Environmental changes have to be made in order to create a barrier-free learning
  environment for all students to access this lesson
• Comment: Establishing a barrier-free environment allows students to feel safe.
  What becomes critical is for the teacher to understand how significantly important
  a person's emotions are in the educational process. Recognizing the value of
  emotions and providing a safe environment for the student, teachers can encourage
  students to establish classroom rules. (Reference *Setting the Stage: Delivering the
  Plan Using the Learner's Brain Model* for more details.)
  Research has shown that the brain's limbic system, located just above the brain
    stem at the base of the brain, is responsible for our emotional responses. (Refer
    to chapter 1 about the Nature of the Learner.) Neuroscientists have determined
    that new information that comes to the brain is processed first in the emotional
    center before being processed in the cognitive center, located in the frontal
    lobe of the cerebrum. With information processing short-circuited first to the
    emotional center, chronic stress may impair long-term memory and learning.
    The effects of stress and learning have significant implications for educators.
  Research has also shown that while threats impede learning, positive emotional
    experiences, during which the brain produces certain chemicals or
    neurotransmitters, can contribute to long-term memory. As stated earlier, all
    education is emotional.
Student Empowerment Program: It is during this phase of instruction that the teacher
  "releases the student" so she can take charge of her learning. The teacher reminds
  the student to use the resources in the room to self-regulate and the rubrics to
  assess their learning.
• For students who still have trouble accessing the lesson, accommodations are made

Readiness Set is to promote sense and meaning (reference *Setting the Stage: Delivering the Plan Using the Learner's Brain Model*) by linking the student's prior knowledge to new knowledge.

Inclusive Teaching Strategies: In order to increase access, content and material will be presented in a variety of ways. Worksheets will be provided and actual fruits will be brought into class to be manipulated and measured. Physical diagrams will be created and modeled to demonstrate the layers of the rainforest. iPads will be used to show actual rainforests throughout the world.

Comments: The brain processes information through the various senses and stores the information in a variety of sections. Hence a multisensory approach helps learners process information via their preferred learning style.

Groupings: Students will be grouped heterogeneously in small groups. Students will have the opportunity to work together in a collaborative learning environment, creating diagrams on the levels of the rainforest as well as measuring and comparing fruits together.

Table 7.3 Whole class procedures

Time	Procedure for the Whole Class	Individual Student/IEP Considerations
10 mins	Readiness Set • Students will be asked what they know about rainforests. • Students will then be asked to gather on the rug and listen to the story *The Great Kapok Tree: A Tale of the Amazon Rain Forest* by Lynne Cherry. • After reading this particular children's book, students will be interested in the topic of rainforests and why they are important to conserve. Comments: The readiness set has been deemed indispensable by many theorists as enumerated by the research. The readiness set is the hook to get students' interest; it sets the stage for learning and focuses the brain to ready itself for the "main attraction." The readiness set also adds meaning to the upcoming lesson.	All students will be sitting near the teacher. The teacher will speak slowly and clearly enough for everyone to understand. There will be some specific breaks or pauses in the story to allow students to discuss in the class so he or she can hear better. The teacher will question students and monitor their progress on what they are thinking and how they feel. The teacher will incorporate some Spanish words in the story as well, so students like Lucy can have a better understanding. Josh and other students will be called on to help read the story or turn pages, so they can get up and move around a little.
15 mins	Introduction of New Material • The teacher will begin to explain how there are many different layers to the rainforest. • The teacher will go over each layer of the rainforest using the smart board and iPads. • The teacher will explain how important the rainforest is to humans and many different animals. Students will turn and talk about the information they received. • The teacher will continue to explain how there are many different types of fruits and vegetables in the rainforest and some can be found at different layers. Students will have the opportunity to move to centers throughout the room to complete investigations. Probing questions will be provided to stimulate the research the students will be doing. • Various fruits and vegetables from the rainforest will be introduced and brought to different tables or student groups.	Students will be able to interact with the smart board as well as iPads when being introduced to the new material. The teacher will be walking about to make sure everyone is interacting with the new material and that everyone can hear what he or she is saying. While utilizing the iPads and smart boards, students will be able to be more active and move around exploring the layers of the rainforest. Josh and other students may enjoy being hands-on with the new material which will engage tactile, kinesthetic, visual, and auditory learners alike. Shannon, like the rest of the class, will be able to have information directly in front of her to help her achieve a better understanding.

(Continued)

Table 7.3 Whole class procedures (*Continued*)

Time	Procedure for the Whole Class	Individual Student/IEP Considerations
15 min	Guided Practice/Exploration/Activity • After the introduction of the new material, students will have a basic understanding of the layers of the rainforest and that there are various fruits and vegetables. • For guided practice, students will be asked to estimate the lengths of certain fruits and vegetables and then measure them using rulers to check their work. They will make assumptions about the fruits and vegetables. • Students will then be able to compare and contrast sizes of different fruits and vegetables as well as layers of the rainforest. • Students will rotate groups so they have a chance to measure all the different examples and compare and contrast sizes and research why they are different.	The teacher will remind students that there are rules to follow as they go from activity to activity. Students must also respect the classroom environment and their classmates. Finally, they have the responsibility to be a scholar and focus on their lesson and think like a professional. Students will engage in hands-on activities. They will manipulate and measure several different fruits and vegetables. The rotations around the classroom will allow all students to move around and see and hear all the examples up close and personal. They will have the opportunity to discuss their findings. Having the iPads and smart board will provide access to all students and allow them to interact with diagrams of the rainforest. The hands-on activities will allow students to be engaged and have the information represented in a variety of ways.

10 mins Closure, summary, or sharing:
- A quick follow-up discussion will bring all the students together and share what they learned.
- Students will be asked to share their answers related to measuring the fruits and which one is the biggest.
- Students will be asked to relate what they learned to the story that was previously read in class.
- Finally, students will receive an exit slip that has the layers of the rainforest.

Homework/Follow-Up Activity (if appropriate).
The exit slip will be given out to students to assist comprehension of the lesson and the main takeaways.
In terms of assessment, students will be given the exit slip as well as two worksheets to complete. The worksheets include basic measuring operations as well as a blank diagram of rainforest layers to be identified and labeled. This will serve as a basic formative assessment; however, students will be informally assessed based on their participation and involvement during the lesson. To reinforce the material and concepts, iPad applications can be used to demonstrate rainforest layers as well as where they are located in the world and why they are important to conserve.

Comment: Closure is also an important process for the learner because the learner will summarize what has been learned and engage in the process of attaching sense and meaning to the learned information. The summary by the student will provide information to the teacher who can ask clarifying questions to the student to help them see relationships and develop understanding.

Student Empowerment Program
promotes student reflection after the lesson so students can determine what worked, what they learned, what they still need to know, and how to adjust their learning.

Closure at the end of a lesson for consolidation (called consolidation closure). The purpose is to ensure that the students are leaving with the correct information and that is why it is called closure for consolidation. The process begins again with the planning stage based upon student information.

Comments: Cooperative learning should be constructed for a purpose not where students are doing a project or activity in a group. It is ineffective when it is not purposeful, planned, and guided. An activity which is not planned is an activity; an activity which is planned is a purposeful activity because it will lead to something.

Comment: Closure provides important feedback for both the teacher and the student. During Closure, the activity assigned to the student by the teacher provides the teacher feedback about the lesson taught. It will give the teacher an idea of whether additional practice time is needed, if the lesson needs to be retaught, or if it is okay to move onto the next concept. After closure, if the objective was mastered, the teacher can then make the decision to move on to a new objective.

Even more important is student reflection.

Index

Note: *Italic* page number refer to figures and tables.

About the Author

Mario C. Barbiere, Ed.D, has decades of experience in the practical application of educational administration and the research foundation associated with it.

His practical knowledge stems from working at all administrative school and district levels including vice principal, principal, assistant superintendent, and superintendent. He has also done extensive work in school turnaround working for the state of New Jersey. He served as Network Turnaround Officer for two large inner city high schools in Newark, New Jersey, which were the fourth and fifth lowest-performing schools in the state. Working with the principal, administrators, and teachers, both schools doubled their test scores in one year and became high achieving schools.

He continued the school turnaround work for the state of New Jersey when New Jersey got a waiver from No Child Left Behind to implement Regional Achievement Centers to work with low-performing schools or schools that had an achievement gap. He served as executive director for Regional Achievement Center, Region 5, overseeing schools in three counties. All schools exited status.

Under the Every Student Succeed Act (ESSA), the Regional Achievement Centers were identified as Comprehensive Support and Improvement Teams (CSI) and Dr. Barbiere was the regional executive director for CSI 3 covering seven counties in New Jersey. His schools exited status.

His doctoral studies at Rutgers University were in Curriculum Theory and Development. His doctorate from Seton Hall University focused on brain research and lesson design. Using that research, he was able to write two books on brain research and lesson design and two books on brain research and instructional delivery. He also worked with Ms. Jane Waitr on a book about student empowerment and early childhood education. All books are available from Rowman & Littlefield.

He was an associate professor at Bloomfield College in the Education Department. He has also taught all the courses required for school supervision and for principal certification for Kean University.

Dr. Barbiere is passionate about teaching and student empowerment; he strives to enable students to be self-dependent and not teacher or school dependent. His decades of experience in the field have resulted in developing rubrics for all phases of instructional planning and delivery, which were field tested and included in his books.

CPSIA information can be obtained
at www.ICGtesting.com
Printed in the USA
BVHW041047200123
656713BV00006B/110

9 781475 864472